ANNOUNCING T
NOW REAI

The edition of *The Complete Work*

Volume I *Behold Your King: The Complete Poetical Works of Frances Ridley Havergal*

Volume II *Whose I Am and Whom I Serve: Prose Works of Frances Ridley Havergal*

Volume III *Loving Messages for the Little Ones: Works for Children by Frances Ridley Havergal*

Volume IV *Love for Love: Frances Ridley Havergal: Memorials, Letters and Biographical Works*

Volume V *Songs of Truth and Love: Music by Frances Ridley Havergal and William Henry Havergal*

David L. Chalkley, Editor Dr. Glen T. Wegge, Music Editor

The Music of Frances Ridley Havergal by Glen T. Wegge, Ph.D.

This Companion Volume to the Havergal edition is a valuable presentation of F.R.H.'s extant scores. Except for a very few of her hymntunes published in hymnbooks, most or nearly all of F.R.H.'s scores have been very little—if any at all—seen, or even known of, for nearly a century. What a valuable body of music has been unknown for so long and is now made available to many. Dr. Wegge completed his Ph.D. in Music Theory at Indiana University at Bloomington, and his diligence and thoroughness in this volume are obvious. First an analysis of F.R.H.'s compositions is given, an essay that both addresses the most advanced musicians and also reaches those who are untrained in music; then all the extant scores that have been found are newly typeset, with complete texts for each score and extensive indices at the end of the book. This volume presents F.R.H.'s music in newly typeset scores diligently prepared by Dr. Wegge, and Volume V of the Havergal edition presents the scores in facsimile, the original 19th century scores. (The essay—a dissertation—analysing her scores is given the same both in this Companion Volume and in Volume V of the Havergal edition.)

Dr. Wegge is also preparing all of these scores for publication in performance folio editions.

This is a magnified portion of the most famous photograph of Frances Ridley Havergal, one of eight of her taken by the prestigious portrait photographers Elliott and Fry in London on Saturday, February 1, 1879, only seven weeks after her 42nd birthday and four months before her unexpected early death on June 3. No one thought that she would die so young.

Under His Shadow.

BY

Frances Ridley Havergal

Taken from the New Edition of

The Complete Works of Frances Ridley Havergal

" Knowing her intense desire that Christ should be magnified, whether
by her life or in her death, may it be to His glory
that in these pages she, being dead,
'Yet speaketh!' "

ISBN 978-1-937236-54-0 Library of Congress: 2016918254

Cover Design by Glen T. Wegge.

Havergal, Frances Ridley
Under His Shadow taken from the edition of the complete works of Frances Ridley Havergal / Frances Ridley Havergal.

1. Havergal, Frances Ridley, 1836–1879. 2. Christian Life. 3. Christian Poetry, English. 4. Music. I. Title

Printed in the United States of America.

This book is printed on acid-free paper.

This is taken from the new edition of *The Complete Works of Frances Ridley Havergal* edited by David L. Chalkley, and Dr. Glen T. Wegge, Music Editor.

In all that she did, and in all that she wrote, Frances Ridley Havergal's one overriding desire was—as Colossians 1:18 says—"that in all things he [*her Lord*] might have the pre-eminence." She saw herself as an instrument in her Saviour's hand, writing for His sake, His glory alone. Indeed the words of Psalm 45:1 were true of her: "My heart is inditing a good matter: I speak of the things which I have made touching the King: my tongue is the pen of a ready writer."

The truth of Christ, which she so loved, and which He used her to present to others, is what is relevant and important, not Frances herself. Understanding the truth of this, you don't first of all think "what a wonderful, fine lady she was" but "what a Saviour ! she had." Jesus Christ alone was changing her from what she was, to become daily more like Himself. Frances would not want anyone to look solely or primarily at her, but she would want all to see her Lord and Saviour. He was her only beauty, righteousness, wisdom, her all. So as you embark on reading, may you too see the Lord Jesus Christ. To see her King is what she would have wanted, the true conclusion of her works and life, and of any genuine disciple's works and life. The Lamb is all the glory in Emmanuel's land, the kingdom of God.

CONTENTS.

LIST OF ILLUSTRATIONS

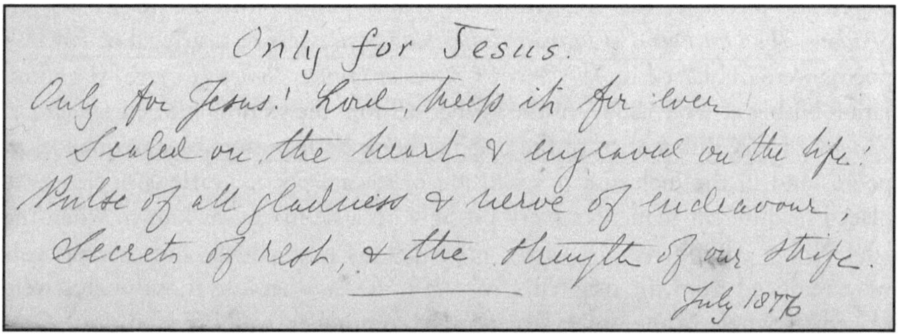

Only for Jesus.

Only for Jesus! Lord, keep it for ever
Sealed on the heart & engraved on the life!
Pulse of all gladness & nerve of endeavour,
Secret of rest, & the strength of our strife.

July 1876

F.R.H.'s manuscript of the single stanza poem "Only for Jesus." See page 51 of this book.

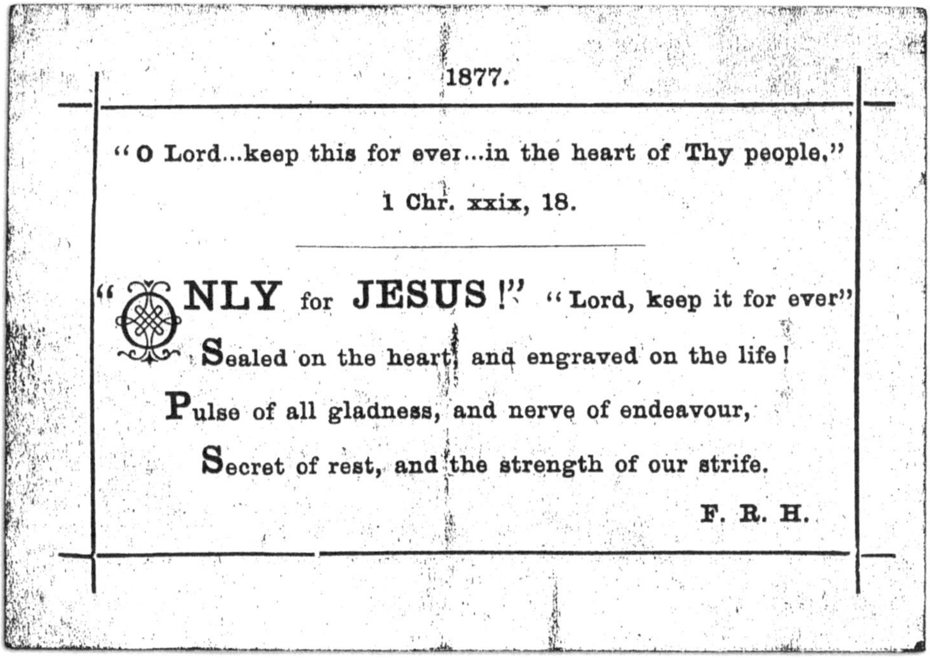

1877.

"O Lord...keep this for ever...in the heart of Thy people."
1 Chr. xxix, 18.

"ONLY for JESUS!" "Lord, keep it for ever"
Sealed on the heart, and engraved on the life!
Pulse of all gladness, and nerve of endeavour,
Secret of rest, and the strength of our strife.

F. R. H.

This card was found among Havergal manuscripts and papers, inexpensive and easy to give to many.

Under His Shadow.

Frances Ridley Havergal published three books of poetry, *The Ministry of Song* (1869), *Under His Shadow* (1874), and *Loyal Responses* (1878). She had not finished her next book of poems when she died on June 3, 1879; in her final illness, she and her sister Maria discussed this book, and Maria posthumously edited and published this collection later that same year with the title *Under His Shadow The Last Poems of Frances Ridley Havergal.* Most or nearly all of F.R.H.'s poems were published in *The Poetical Works of Frances Ridley Havergal* (London: James Nisbet & Co., 1884). In the Nisbet edition, the section entitled *Under His Shadow* is very different from the original book both in the order (sequence) of poems and in the inclusion or exclusion of several poems: various poems were placed in different sequences (very possibly because more was known when the later Nisbet edition was prepared), other poems were added, and other poems were removed from the original *Under His Shadow* (because those poems were placed elsewhere in the much larger, more comprehensive Nisbet edition). This is not said to disparage the Nisbet *Poetical Works* edition at all: that is a sterling compilation, very finely prepared. Very possibly or likely Maria realized more (about titles, sequences, texts, etc.) after the original *Under His Shadow* was published and before the finalized Nisbet edition was published. This is said to explain that this small volume of *Under His Shadow* follows the original 1879 sequence (placement of the poems) of that book, though the titles and texts of the individual poems in the 1884 Nisbet edition (later prepared, and likely more accurate than the earlier, original book) are copied here.

David L. Chalkley and Dr. Glen T. Wegge, November, 2016

Next is the original Preface to *Under His Shadow*.

PREFACE.

My dear sister Frances had intended writing an opening poem to this volume, showing why she chose its title of

"Under His Shadow."

Only these fragmentary lines, written in pencil, were found:—

"Faint footsteps tracked the burning sand
Far o'er the wild white waste,
A thirsting band, lessening each hour;
Lost was all energy for hopeful haste,
Lost e'en despair's convulsive power,

Although the dangerous glare
Fell fiercely through heat-quivering air.
Although the way was strewn with bleaching bones,
And treasure dropped by hands that could not care
For gold or precious stones ;
When very life evaporated, and although
There was no safety in that terrible plain.
No point of pause, but death. For swift or slow.
Advance or halt, seemed all alike in vain:—

* * * * *

Happily I have preserved in writing the recollection of a conversation, in which she gave me an outline of what she intended the volume to be.

Three years ago, when we were in Switzerland, and she was recovering from illness, she said to me: "Marie, I think my third volume of poems will be my 'Nunc Dimittis' ! Do you remember my poem, 'Threefold Praise'? I think my first volume, 'Ministry of Song,' was like Haydn; then 'Under the Surface' like Mendelssohn; and I want my third volume to be 'Messiah' all to His praise!

"I should like the title to be 'Under His Shadow.' I seem to see four pictures suggested by that: under the shadow of a rock in a weary plain; under the shadow of a tree; closer still, under the shadow ot His wing ; nearest and closest, in the shadow of His hand. Surely that hand must be the pierced hand, that may oftentimes press us sorely, and yet evermore encircling, upholding, and shadowing!"

Only the day before my dear sister died she asked me to collect and publish all her MS. poems. I said, "Shall the title be 'Under His Shadow'?" and she answered: "Oh, yes; I am so glad you remembered it."

And now she more than realizes her own words:

"As we fall o'erawed
Upon our faces, and are lifted higher
By His great gentleness, and carried nigher
Than unredeemed angels, till we stand
Even *in* the hollow of His hand:
Nay, more ! we lean upon His breast;
There, there we find a point of perfect rest
And glorious safety!"

Maria V. G. Havergal.

Oakhampton, Stourport,
November, 1879.

An Easter Prayer

Oh let me know
The power of Thy Resurrection;
Oh let me show
Thy risen life in calm and clear reflection;
Oh let me soar
Where Thou, my Saviour Christ art gone before;
In mind and heart
Let me dwell always, only, where Thou art.

Oh let me give
Out of the gifts Thou freely givest;
Oh let me live
With life abundantly because Thou livest;
Oh make me shine
In darkest places for Thy light is mine;
Oh let me be
A faithful witness for Thy truth and Thee.

Oh let me show
The strong reality of Gospel story;
Oh let me go
From strength to strength, from glory unto glory;
Oh let me sing
For very joy because Thou art my King
Oh let me praise
Thy love and faithfulness through all my days.

F.R.H.'s fair copy autograph, very late in her life, found in her last Manuscript Book, № IX. *See page 112 of this book.*

'Under His Shadow.'

An Interlude.

THAT part is finished! I lay down my pen,
And wonder if the thoughts will flow as fast
Through the more difficult defile. For the last
Was easy, and the channel deeper then.
My Master, I will trust Thee for the rest;
Give me just what Thou wilt, and that will be my best.

How can *I* tell the varied, hidden need
Of Thy dear children, all unknown to me,
Who at some future time may come and read
What I have written! All are known to Thee.
As Thou hast helped me, help me to the end;
Give me Thy own sweet messages of love to send.

So now, I pray Thee, keep my hand in Thine,
And guide it as Thou wilt. I do not ask
To understand the wherefore of each line;
Mine is the sweeter, easier, happier task
Just to look up to Thee for every word,
Rest in Thy love, and trust, and know that I am heard.

The Thoughts of God.

THY thoughts, O God! O theme Divine!
Except Thy Spirit in my darkness shine,
And make it light,
And overshadow me
With stilling might,
And touch my lips that I may speak of Thee,—
How shall I soar
To thoughts of Thy thoughts? and how dare to write
Of Thine?

Thou understandest mine
Far off and long before.
Thou searchest, knowest, compassest! Thy hand is laid
Upon me. Whither shall I flee
From Omnipresence and Omniscience? If I fly
To heaven, Thou art there: and if I lie
In the unseen land,
Behold, Thou art there also! If I take
The wings of morning, and my dwelling make
In the uttermost parts of the great sea,
Even there Thy hand shall lead me, Thy right hand
Shall hold me. If I say
Surely the night
Shall cover me, it shall be light
About me. Yea, the shade
Of darkness hideth not from Thee,
Night shineth as the day;
The darkness and the light are both alike to Thee.

Thee I will praise: for I am fearfully
And wonderfully made.
My substance was not hid from Thee
When I was made in secret, curiously wrought
And yet imperfect. Then
Thine eyes did see me. In Thy book
Were all my members written, when
Not one of them was into being brought.
Such knowledge is too wonderful for me,
Too excellent, too high. Yet 'tis but one
Keen ray of Thy great sun
Touching an atom in a dusty nook!

One ray! while others traverse depths profound
Of possible chaos; and illume
The boundless bound
Of space; and vivify worlds all unguessed,
To whom
Our farthest eastern spark,
Caught by the mightiest telescope that ever pierced the dark,
Is farthest west.

One ray! while others overflow
The countless hosts of angels with celestial blaze;
With still diviner glow,
Flooding each heart with adoration sweet;
And yet too glorious for the gaze
Of seraphim, who cover face and feet
With burning wings,
While through the universe their 'Holy, holy,' rings.

Only one ray! Yet doth it come
So close to us, so very near,
Our inmost selves enfolding,
Discerning, penetrating,—we, beholding
Its terrible brightness, well might fear,
But for the glow
Of known and trusted Love that pulseth warm below
And so
The psalm ariseth, strong and clear,
'How precious are Thy thoughts to me, O God!
How great their sum!'
Uncounted, marvellous, and very deep and broad,
Unsearchable and high!
Infinity
Of holiest, mightiest mystery,
That never sight
Or tongue of mortal seer
Could see or tell,
That never flight
Of flame-like spirits that in strength excel
Hath reached! The very faith that brings us near
Reveals new distances, new depths of light
Unfathomed,—seas of suns that never eye
Created, hath beheld or ever can behold!
What know we of God's thoughts? One word of gold
A volume doth enfold.
They are—'Not ours!'
Ours? what are they? their value and their powers?
So evanescent, that while thousands fleet

Across the busy brain,
Only a few remain
To set their seal on memory's strange consistence.
Of these, some worthless, some a life-regret,
That we would fain forget;
And very few are rich and great and sweet;
And fewer still are lasting gain,
And these most often born of pain,
Or sprung from strong concussion into strong existence.

What else? Even in their proudest strength so weak,
So isolated and so rootless,
So flowerless and so fruitless;—
We think, and dare not do,—we think, and cannot speak!
A thought alone is less than breath,
Only the shudder of a living death,
A thing of scorn,
A formless embryo in chaos born,
It must be seized with resolute grasp of will,
With swiftness and with skill,
And moulded on life's anvil, ere it glow
With any fire or force;
And wrought with many a blow
And welded in the heat by toiling strength
With many another, ere it go at length
The humblest mission to fulfil.
And then its tiny might
Is not inherent, but alone dependent
Upon the primal source
And spring of power, First, Sole, Supreme, Transcendent!

What else? So circumscribed in flight!
Like bats in sunshine, striking helpless wings
Against the shining things,
That to their dazzled sight
Appear not; hindered everywhere
By unseen obstacles with puzzling pain.
Or like the traveller, toiling long to gain

An Alpine summit, white and fair,
With far-extending view; but still withheld,
And to the downward track with fainting step compelled
By an intangible barrier; for the air
Is all too rare,
Too keenly pure
For valley-dweller to endure.
For thus our thoughts rebound
From the Invisible-Infinite, on every side
Hemmed ever round
By the Impassable, that never mortal pinion
Hath over-soared, that mocks at human pride,
Imprisoned in its own supposed dominion.

What else? So mingled, so impure;
So interwoven with the threads of sin,
Visible or invisible as the sight
Is purged to see them in God's light;
So subtle in their changeful forms, now dark, now bright;
Such mystery of iniquity within,
That we must loathe our very thoughts, but for the cure
He hath devised,—the blessed Tree
The Lord hath shown us, that, cast in, can heal
The fountain whence the bitter waters flow.
Divinest remedy
Whose power we feel,
Whose grace we comprehend not, but we know.

What else? So fallible, so full of errors,—
No certainty! In aught unproved and new,
Treading volcanic soil o'er smothered terrors;
Spectral misgivings rising to the view,
As each step crushes through
Some older crust of truth assumed. And this is all
That human thoughts can do,
Leaning on human strength and reason solely;
Now wrong, now right, now false, now true,
As may befall!

And even the truest never reaching wholly
Truth Absolute,
That still our touch eludes,
And vanishes in deeper depths when man intrudes
Within her awful solitudes,
Where many a string is mute
And many awanting, all the rest
Imperfectly attuned at best,—
We can but wait for truth of tone,
For truth of modulation and expression,
With lowliest confession
Of utter powerlessness, content
To trust His thoughts and not our own,—
Until the Maker of the instrument
Shall tune it in another sphere,
By His own perfect hand and ear.

Now turn we from the darkness to the light,
From dissonance to pure and full accord!
'My thoughts are not as your thoughts, saith the Lord,
Nor are your ways as My ways. As the height
Of heaven above the earth, so are My ways,
My thoughts, to yours;—out of your sight,
Above your praise.'
O oracle most grand!
Thus teaching by sublimest negative
What by a positive we could not understand,
Or, understanding, live!
And now, search fearlessly
The imperfections and obscurity,
The weakness and impurity,
Of all our thoughts. On each discovery
Write, 'NOT as ours!' Then, in every line,
Behold God's glory shine
In humbling yet sweet contrast, as we view
His thoughts, Eternal, Strong, and Holy, Infinite, and True.

And now, what have we of these thoughts of God,
So high, so deep, so broad?

What hath He given, and what are we receiving?
A revelation
Dim, pale, and cold
Beside their hidden fire, yet gorgeously enscrolled
Upon His wide Creation.
He would not all withhold,
His children in the silent darkness leaving;
Nor would He overwhelm our heart
And strike it dumb;
And so He hath enfolded some
In fair expressions for the eye and ear
Though faint, yet clear;
Such as our powers may apprehend in part.
Thus hath He wrought
The dazzling swiftness of the thought
That veiled itself for mortal ken in light.
And thus the myriad-handed might
Of that from which the million-teeming ocean fell,
No greater toil to Him,
From silent depth to surfy rim,
Than the small crystal drop which fills a rosy shell.
And thus the Infinite Ideal
Of perfect Beauty, (only real
In Him and through Him, pure conception
Too exquisite for our perception,)
He hath translated, giving us such lines
As we can trace,
In mountain grandeur and in lily grace,
In sunset, cloudland, or soul-moulded face,
Such alphabets and signs
As we, His little ones, may slowly, softly read,
Supplying thus a deep, true spirit-need.

What know we more? One thought He hath expressed
In that great scheme
Of which we, straining, catch a glimpse or gleam
In light or shadow;—scheme embracing all,
Star-system cycles and the sparrow's fall;—
Scheme all-combining, wisest, grandest, best.

We call it Providence. And each may deem
Himself a tiny centre of that thought;
For how mysteriously enwrought
Are all our moments in its folds of might,
Our own horizon ever bounding
And yet not limiting, but still surrounding
Our lives, while reaching far beyond our quickest sight.
O thought of consummated harmony!
Each life is one note in that symphony,
Without which were its cadence incomplete:
Yet each note complex, formed of many a reed;
And each reed quivering with vibrations passing count,
And each vibration blending
In mystic trinities ascending
Through weird harmonics that recede
Into the unknown silences, or meet
In dashing thrills unanalyzed, and mount
In tangled music, yet all plain and clear
Unto the Master's ear.
O thought of consummated melody
And perfect rhythm! though its mighty beat
Transcend angelic faculty,
And though its mighty bars
May be the fall of worlds, the birth of stars,
Its measure—all eternity—
One echo, calm and sweet,
Our clue to this great music of God's plan,
Sounds on in ever-varying repeat—
Glory to God on high, peace and goodwill to man!

What have we more? Scan we the blinding blaze
Of the refulgent rays
Outpourèd from the Very Fount of Light?
One thought of God in undiluted splendour
Flashed on our feeble gaze,
Were never borne by mortal sight.
He knew it, and He gave,
In mercy tender,

All that the soul unwittingly doth crave,
All that it can receive. He robed
In finite words the sparkles of His thought,
The starry fire englobed
In tiny spheres of language, shielding, softening thus
The living, burning glory. And He brought
Even to us
This strange celestial treasure that no prayer
Had asked of Him, no ear had heard,
No heart of man conceived. He laid it there,
Even at our feet, and said it was His Word.
O mystery of tender grace!
We find
God's thoughts in human words enshrined,
God's very life and love with ours entwined.
All wonderingly from page to page we pass,
Owning the darkening yet revealing glass;
In every line we trace,
In fair display,
Prismatic atoms of the glorious bow
Projected on the darkest cloud that e'er
O'ergloomed the world that God had made so fair,
The rainbow of His covenant; each one
Reflecting perfectly a sevenfold ray,
Shot from the sun
Of His exceeding love,
Strong and serene above,
Upon a tremulous drop of tearful life below.

One thought, His thought of thoughts, awakes our song
Of endless thanks and marvelling adoration
More than aught else. For Providence, Creation,
All He hath made and all He doth prepare,
Thoughts grand and wise, and strong,
Thoughts tender and most fair,
Are pale beside the glory of Salvation,
Redemption's gracious plan and glorious revelation:—

The focus where all rays unite;
Each attribute arrayed in sevenfold light,
Each adding splendour to the rest.
The meeting blest
Of His great love and foreseen human woe
Struck forth a mighty fire, that sent a glow
Throughout the universe;—an overflow
To the dim confines that none know
Save He who traced them; lit up gloriously
The farthest vistas of Eternity;
And, flooding heaven itself with radiance new,
Revealed the heart of God, all-merciful, all-true.

Thus are the thoughts of God made known to men.
Yet is all revelation bounded
First by its vehicle, and then
By its reception. Unseen things
Remain unfathomed and unsounded,
And hidden as the springs
Of an immeasurable sea,
Because His thought, sublime and great,
No language finds commensurate
With its infinity;
And when compressed in any finite mould,
'Tis but a fraction that the mind of man
Receiveth. For we hold
But what we span,
We only see
What feeble lenses and weak sight may scan.
And thus a double lessening, double veiling
Of the unimagined glory of a thought of Him
Who dwells between the cherubim!
First, suffering and paling
By its necessitate transition
From Infinite to Finite, for that all expression
Is by its nature finite; then the vision
Which angels might receive straightway,
Unshorn of any ray,
And hold in full possession,

Must enter by the portal
Of faculties sin-paralyzed and mortal;
And in the human breast's low-vaulted gloom
It finds no room
For any high display.

This is no guess-work. It is even so
With our poor thoughts. For they are always more
Than any form or language can convey.
We know
Things that we cannot say;
We soar,
Where we could never map our flight.
We see
Flashes and colourings too quick and bright
For any hand to paint. We meet
Depths that no line can sound. We hear
Strange far-off mental music, all too sweet,
Too great for any earthly instrument;
Gone, if we strive to bring it near.

For who that knows
The sudden surging and the startling throes
Of subterranean soul-fires with no vent,
That seek an Etna all in vain;—
Or the slow forming of some grand, fair thought,
With exquisite lingering outwrought,
Only to melt before the touch of effort or of pain:—
(Like quivering rose-fire 'neath a filmy veil
In mountain dawn,
That grows all still and pale
When the transparent silver is withdrawn.)
Oh! who that knows but owns the meagre dower
Of poor weak language married to thought's royal power—
Oh! who that knows but needs must own,
If it be thus
Even with us,

Groping and tottering alone
Around the footstool of His throne,
With limited ideas and babe-like powers,
What must it be with Him, whose thoughts are not as ours!
And now
We only bow,
And gaze above
In raptured awe and silent love;
For mortal speech
Can never reach
A word of meetly-moulded praise,
For one glimpse of the blessèd rays,
Ineffable and purely bright,
Outflowing ever from the Unapproachèd Light.

They say there is a hollow, safe and still,
A point of coolness and repose
Within the centre of a flame, where life might dwell
Unharmed and unconsumed, as in a luminous shell,
Which the bright walls of fire enclose
In breachless splendour, barrier that no foes
Could pass at will.

There is a point of rest
At the great centre of the cyclone's force,
A silence at its secret source;—
A little child might slumber undistressed,
Without the ruffle of one fairy curl,
In that strange central calm amid the mighty whirl.

So, in the centre of these thoughts of God,
Cyclones of power, consuming glory-fire,—
As we fall o'erawed
Upon our faces, and are lifted higher
By His great gentleness, and carried nigher
Than unredeemèd angels, till we stand
Even *in* the hollow of His hand,—

Nay, more! we lean upon His breast—
There, there we find a point of perfect rest
And glorious safety. There we see
His thoughts to usward, thoughts of peace
That stoop to tenderest love; that still increase
With increase of our need; that never change,
That never fail, or falter, or forget.
O pity infinite!
O royal mercy free!
O gentle climax of the depth and height
Of God's most precious thoughts, most wonderful, most strange!
'For I am poor and needy, yet
The Lord Himself, Jehovah, *thinketh upon me!*'

Zenith.

I.

We watched the gradual rising of a star,
Whose delicate, clear ray outshone the crowd;
Gleaming between the rifts of parting cloud,
Brighter above each dusky-veiling bar.
The fairy child, the glimpse of girlish face,
Rising to woman's dower of fairest, fullest grace.

And still she rose, and still she calmly shone,
Walking in brightness ever-brightening still;
Gladdening, attracting at her queenly will,
With starlike influence. The years wore on,
And Isabel, the star, the pearl, the flower,
Could not but know her gift, the secret of her power.

'Never so lovely as to-night,' they said,
Again and yet again! There came a night
When many owned afresh the royal might
Of beauty, as she came with snowfall tread,
And summer smile, and simple maiden dress,
Crowned only with the light and her own loveliness.

And the next day she was a little tired;
And the next night the rose had somewhat paled.
The fair pearl glistened, yet it somewhat failed
Of the past gleam, the radiance all-admired.
From the soft emerald of the wind-waved grass,
How soon the diamond sparkle of the dew must pass!

And the next week the sunbeams vainly sought
An entrance, where their merry rival lay
Fevered and weary; while, from day to day,
The quick pulse wasted what short slumber brought
Of slow renewing. So the dark mist fell,
And hid the starry fire that all had loved so well.

Again she shone, when from that dark mist freed,
But with that singular radiance never more;
The brightening upward path so quickly o'er,
The solemn westward curve begun indeed!
The unconscious zenith of her lovely light
For ever left behind on that gay triumph-night!

II.

Ho! for the Alps! The weary plains of France,
And the night-shadows, leaving far behind,
For pearl horizons with pure summits lined,—
On through the Jura-gorge, in swift advance
Speeds Arthur, with keen hope and buoyant glee,
On to the mountain land, home of the strong and free!

On! to the morning flush of gold and rose;
On! to the torrent and the hoary pine;
On! to the stillness of life's utmost line;
On! to the crimson fire of sunset snows.
Short starlit rest, then with the dawn's first streak,
On! to the silent crown of some lone icy peak!

'Twas no nerve-straining effort, then, for him
To emulate the chamois-hunter's leap
Across the wide rock-chasm, or the deep
And darkly blue crevasse with treacherous rim,

Or climb the sharp arête, or slope of snow,
With Titan towers above, and cloud-filled gulfs below.

It was no weariness or toil to count
Hour after hour in that weird white realm,
With guide of Alp-renown to touch the helm
Of practised instinct, rocky spires to mount,
Or track the steepest glacier's fissured length,
In the abounding joy of his unconquered strength.

But it was gladness none can realize
Who have not felt the wild Excelsior thrill,
The strange exhilarate energies that fill
The bounding pulses, as the intenser skies
Embrace the infinite whiteness, clear and fair,
Inhaling vigorous life with that quick crystal air.

That Alpine witchery still onward lures,
Upward, still upward, till the fatal list
Grows longer of the early mourned and missed;
Leading where surest foot no more ensures
The life that is not ours to throw away
For the exciting joys of one brief summer day.

For there are sudden dangers none foreknow;
The scarlet-threaded rope can never mock
The sound-loosed avalanche, frost-cloven rock,
Or whirling storm of paralyzing snow.
But Arthur's foot was kept; no deathward slips
Darkened the zenith of his strength with dire eclipse.

So year by year, as his rich manhood filled,
He revelled in health-giving mountain feats;
Spurning the trodden tracks and curious streets,
As fit for old men, and for boys unskilled
In Alpine arts, not strong nor bold enough
To battle with the blast and scale the granite bluff.

One glowing August sun went forth in might,
And smote with rosy sword each snowy brow,
Bright accolade of grandeur! Now, oh now
Amid that dazzling wealth of purest light,

His long ambition should be crowned at last,
And every former goal rejoicingly o'erpast.

For ere the white fields softened in the glow,
He stood upon a long-wooed virgin-peak,
One of the few fair prizes left to seek;
Each rival pinnacle left far below!
He stood in triumph on the conquered height:
And yet a shadow fell upon his first delight.

For well he knew that he had surely done
His utmost, and that never summer day
Could bring a moment on its radiant way
Like the first freshness of that conquest, won
Where all had lost before. A sudden tear
Veiled all the glorious view, so grand, so calm, so clear!

III.

An hour of song! of musical delight
To those whose quick, instructed ear could trace,
Through complex harmonies, the artistic grace,
The finest shades of meaning, and the might
Of order and of law. Nor less to those
Who loved it as we love the fragrance of the rose.

And Cecil stood, with all the added ease
Of ripe experience and of sure success;
With all her glad instinctive consciousness
Of natural gift that could not fail to please;
With all her rich maturity of tone,
Like sun-glow of the South on purple clusters thrown.

She sang rejoicing in her song,—each bar
A separate pulse of pleasure. Were there none
To listen and applaud, or only one,
As freely she had poured it. For a star
Shines, not because we watch it! Only blaze
Of artificial light reserves its measured rays.

Yet who, that ever tasted, does not know
The witchery of any phase of power,
Ascendency unsought, magnetic dower
Of influence? And Cecil found it so,
And though but vaguely conscious of her might,
Lived in her own strong spell, a glamour of delight.

Nor only joy of power and joy of song
To fill the singer's chalice were combined
But sympathetic influences of mind
Acting, re-acting, as the charmèd throng
Followed the wave of her swift magic wand,
Yet lured her ever on to fair heights still beyond.

And so the song passed to its dying fall,
As the electric interchanges crossed.
What marvel that the closing chord was lost
In rush of quick applause and fond recall!
And Cecil rose once more, and poured again,
From fuller-gushing fount, the doubly welcomed strain.

Higher and higher rose the glorious song,
Deeper and deeper grew the silence round;
All unrestrained the free, full notes resound,
In splendid carol-gladness, holding long
Unwearied listeners in chains unseen,
As willing captives led by their victorious queen.

Tribute of wondering smile was freely paid,
And then, as subtle modulation wrought
Soft shadows in the sunny strain, some brought
The deeper homage of a tear, and, swayed
Beyond confession, strove in vain to hide
The unconquerable rush of sweet emotion's tide.

Then once again the clear tones rose and swelled,
While flashed the singer's eye with inward fire,
And still the spirit of the song soared higher
Until the closing cadence, as she held
All hearts entranced, till like a sunset ray,
The last, long, sweet note thrilled, and softly died away.

And all was over! Ah, she had not guessed
That she had touched the zenith of her song,
That gradual declining, slow and long
Must mark the path now trending to the west!
No boundary line is seen, and yet we cross
In one veiled hour, from gain, to sure though lingering loss.

She often sang again. But oftener fell
Apologies of unaffected truth.
There was more effort, yet less power, in sooth;
The ringing tone less like a golden bell.
Not quite in voice of late. 'I'll do my best!
Do not expect too much;—I think my voice needs rest.'

So one by one the songs no more were seen
That called for grandest tone and clearest trill.
And when she sang, though old friends loved it still,
The stranger wondered what the spell had been.
And then they spoke of how she *used* to sing!
Passing, or passed away is every earthly thing.

IV.

A silent house beneath a dome of stars,
A deeply-shaded lamp, a lonely room;
A fire whose fitful whispers through the gloom
In rhythmic cadence leapt athwart the bars:
A broad, worn desk; a broad, worn, bending brow;
Yet a bright eye beneath, full of strange brightness now.

A rapid hand, that wrote swift words of flame,
Far-glowing words to kindle other fires;
Words that might flash along Time's mystic wires,
And thrill the ages with a deathless name;
Barbed words, that fasten where they fall, and stay
Deep in the souls of men, and never pass away.

Little recked Theodore of fame that night
And less of gold. The current was too strong

For such vain barques to launch. It swept along
Whither he hardly knew; the impulse bright
Passing at every turn some opening view,
Some echoing mountain height, some vista far and new.

Lost memories trooped in amid the crowd
Of happiest images; ethereal forms
Of weirdly prescient fancy, spectral swarms,
Before him in oppressive beauty bowed,
And beckoned him, with gleaming hands, to grasp
Their fleeting loveliness in firm and joyous clasp.

And inward music rose, and wreathed around
Each thought that shaped itself to outline clear;
The royal chimes rang on, more sweet, more near,
With every gust. He caught the silver sound,
And cast its fairy mantle o'er the flow
Of his melodious lines, in all their fiery glow.

Such times are but the crystallizing hours
That make the rainbow-bearing prism. They change
Long-seething soul-solutions into strange
And startling form;—new properties and powers,
And beauties hardly dreamt, yet latent there,
The poet-touch evokes, strong, marvellous, and fair.

For there are long, slow overtures before
Such bursts of song;—much tension unconfessed,
Much training and much tuning,—years compressed,
Concentrated in ever-filling store;
Till thoughts, that surged in secret deep below,
Rise from volcanic fount in sudden overflow.

Much living to short writing! such the law
Of living poems, that have force to reach
Depths that are sounded by no surface-speech,
And thence the sympathetic waters draw
With golden chain of many a fire-forged link,
Gently, yet mightily, up to the pearly brink.

Was it the stillness of the lonely night
That set his spirit free, with wizard hand,
Opening the gates of more than fairyland?
Oft had he known the pulse of poet-might,
But never quite the free, exultant power
In which he revelled now through that enchanted hour.

Was it not rather that the harvest-time,
After the sowing and the watering long,
Was fully come; the golden sheaves of song
Falling in fulness, and that royal chime
Pealing the harvest-home of wealth unseen,
Where the remaining years might only come and glean?

At length the last page lay beneath the light,
From wavering erasure free, and wrought
Too perfectly for any after-thought.
He rose, threw up the sash, and on the night,—
The brilliant, solemn night,—looked forth and sighed,
And felt the immediate ebb of that unwonted tide.

For it was over! and the work was done
For which his life was lived! unconscious yet!
The blossom fell because the fruit was set;
The standard furled because the field was won.
And with the energy, the gladness passed,
And left him wearied out and sorrowful at last.

For only work that is for God alone
Hath an unceasing guerdon of delight,
A guerdon unaffected by the sight
Of great success, nor by its loss o'erthrown.
All else is vanity beneath the sun,
There may be joy in *doing*, but it palls when *done.*

V.

Once more. A battle-field of mental might,
A broad arena for the utmost skill
Of world-famed gladiators, echoing still
With praise or cruel blame, beyond the sight

Of each day's keen spectators, to the verge
Of widest continents and ocean's farthest surge.

A great arena, whence the issues flow
Not only through an empire but a world,
Moulding the centuries; wherein are hurled
Thunders whose ultimate havoc none can know,
Striking not names but nations:—such the scene
Of conflict and renown, long entered by Eugene.

Many a time his weighty sword he threw
Into the scale of victory, and swayed
The critical turns, the great events that made
The era's history. For well he knew
Each subtle art of eloquence, combined
With rarest gifts of speech, and native powers of mind.

His patriotism earned a noble meed
Of trust and honour, more than any fame,
And sweeter. Yet some thought his hard-won claim
Not meetly recognised. Perchance indeed
The shadow crossed his own thought, as he found
Less kingly orators with heavier laurels crowned.

At length a contest of long doubtful end
Drew to a climax, and his soul was stirred,
And every generous faculty was spurred
To utmost energy. For he could spend
His very self upon the cause that seemed
Clear justice and clear right; or rather, so he deemed!

For there are few who care to analyze
The mingled motives, in their complex force,
Of some apparently quite simple course.
One disentangled skein might well surprise.
Perhaps a 'single heart' is *never* known
Save in the yielded life that lives for God alone,—

And that is *therefore* doubted, as a dream,
By those who know not the tremendous power

Of all-constraining love! So in that hour
Of fierce excitement, 'mid the flashing gleam
Of measured glaive, I will not dare to say
That Eugene's purest zeal no party claim might sway.

Still, all combined to bid the eagle soar
Beyond the common clouds, the shifting mists
Of every-day debate, the very lists
Of strong opponents strengthening him the more.
As the strong pinion finds the opposing breeze
The very means of rising over land and seas.[1]

So Eugene rose in his full manly strength,
Reining at first the fiery courser in,
That with calm concentration he might win
The captious ear;—reserve of power at length,
At the right moment from the wise curb freed,
Triumphantly burst forth with grand impetuous speed.

And as the great speech mounted to a pause
Some foes were silenced, some were wholly gained,
And all were spellbound, stilled, and marvel-chained,
And, more than all the clatter of applause,
The cause was won! 'Eugene was at his best
To-night!' So much they knew! They did not know the rest!

For they who watched with envy or delight
The moment of his zenith, little knew
It was the moment of his setting too;
For fell paralysis drew near that night.
Never again Eugene might proudly stand
And sway the men who swayed the sceptre of his land.

VI.

A simple Christmas Day at home! And yet
It was the very zenith of two stars
That rose together through the cloudy bars,
In bright perpetual conjunction met.

[1] See Duke of Argyle's 'Reign of Law.' [Apparently this is *The Reign of Law* by George Douglas Campbell, Duke of Argyll (1823–1900), London: Alexander Strahan, 1867.]

A day whose memory should never cease,—
A Coronation Day of Love and Joy and Peace.

The culmination of two lives that passed
Through many a chance and change of chequered years,
Each shining for the other, hopes and fears
Centred within their home! And now at last
They gazed upon a clear, calm sky around,
And rested in their love, that day serenely crowned.

Bernard and Constance had no wish beyond
Each other's gladness, and the fuller good
Of those belovèd ones who blithely stood
Around the Christmas fire,—the fair and fond,
The strong and merry; sons and daughters grown
In closest unity,—rich treasures all their own.

Bright arrows of full quiver! still unshot
By ruthless bow of Time and scattered wide,
Still in the sweet home-bundle tightly tied,
Though feathered for the flight from that safe spot.
Flight when? and whither? Ah me! who might say
What should befall before another Christmas Day!

Closer they clustered in the twilight fall,
And talked of pleasant memories of the year,
And then of pleasant prospects far and near;
Each name responding at each gleeful call.
The merry mention of a dear name there
Had never yet been hushed by any empty chair.

But, most of all, the gladness and the pride
Circled around the eldest brother's name;
His first success, his rising college fame,
Made merriest music at that warm fireside;
And in the parent-hearts deep echoes thrilled,
As the repeated chord proclaimed fond hopes fulfilled.

No dim presentiment of sorrow fell
Upon that zenith hour of happiness,

Perhaps the brightest that could ever bless
A merely earthly lot; the purest well
Of natural joy, unselfish, undefiled,
Up-springing to the day, while heaven above it smiled.

And so the evening hours sped swiftly by,
And Christmas carols closed the happy time,
And Christmas bells, in sweet wind-wafted chime,
Stole softly through the shutters. Not a sigh
With music of the gay good-night was blent,
No discord in that full, harmonious content.

What then? Bernard and Constance wakeful lay
A long, long while, unwilling each to tell
That, as the midnight tolled, it seemed the knell
Of the great gladness of that Christmas Day.
'Oh, what if it should prove too bright to last,
Clear shining that precedes the wild and rainy blast!'

And they were right. It *could* not come again!
Sickness, and scattering, and varied woe,
Yet nothing but the lot of most below,
Soon marred the music of that perfect strain.
And though the westering path had many a gleam,
That zenith-joy was but an oft-remembered dream.

VII.

A soft spring twilight. Cherry blossoms white
Whispered about the summer they were told
Was coming, when the beech trees would unfold
Their horny buds, and chestnuts would be dight
In great green leaves. 'What will become of us?'
They wondered! And they shivered as they questioned thus.

For the east wind came by, with curfew bell
Upon his wings, and touched them stealthily,
Shrivelling the tender leaves. And silently
In their sweet white array the blossoms fell.

Ah for the zenith of the cherry tree!
Yet *is* it past, although the snowy glories be?

Wait for the shining of the summer day;
Wait for the crimson glow amid the green;
Wait for the wealth of ruby ripeness, seen
After the fitful spring has passed away.
Wait till the Master comes, with His own hand
To find His pleasant fruit in clusters rich and grand.

Yes, soft spring twilight! And a bowing head,
A kneeling form amid the shadows grey;
A heart from which the hopes had passed away,
That made life exquisite as the blossoms shed
Around that open window;—and a throb
Of dull grey pain, that rose, and forced one low deep sob.

Only the zenith of his youth had passed,
And scarcely that. Yet perhaps the saddest time
Is while the echo of the matin chime
Has hardly died away in silence vast;
Sadder to realize the noonday height,
Than the slow-gathering shades of long impending night.

It did not seem that there could ever be
Another zenith, different, and bright
With grander hopes, and far more glorious light
Than all the spells of syren minstrelsy,
And all the love and gladness that entwined
The merry paths of youth, for ever left behind.

For Godfrey had no special powers to spur
To emulation in the great world-race,
No special gifts or aims;—the open space
A possible joy had filled—the dream of her
Who might have been and yet was not to be
Queen of his life! and now—the dark-draped throne was free!

Free! Yet Another claimed that empty throne,
And in the twilight He was drawing near,

'Mid all those shadows of dim grief, and fear,
And sense of vanity. The King unknown,
Unrecognised as yet, was come to reign,
And yet to crown the life that owned its life was vain.

And while the spring airs trembled through the trees,
The gracious Wind that bloweth where it lists
Dispersed the fallacies, the world-breathed mists
That hid unseen realities. That Breeze
Unveiled the mysteries of hidden sin,
And let the all-searching Light flash startlingly within.

Then the vague weariness was roused indeed,
And passed away for ever, as he saw
The nearer lightnings of the holy law
Through suddenly deepening darkness; then the need
More of a Saviour than mere safety dawned
In lurid daybreak, as he glimpsed the gulf that yawned

Close at his feet—those careless feet that trod
So merrily a harmless-seeming course
Of merely useless pleasure, by the force
Of custom, and yet never came to God,
Never yet stepped upon the Living Way
That only leads to life and everlasting day.

Again that holy Breeze swept by in might,
And fanned each faint desire to stronger flame;
He said, 'O bid me come to Thee!' He came,
Just as he was, that memorable night.
And lo! the King, who waited at the door,
Entered, to save, to reign, and to go out no more.

And then he saw those awful lightnings fall
Through the cleft heavens upon a lonely Tree
That stood upon a mount called Calvary,
And knew that stroke had spent the fiery ball:
And then the earthquake closed the gulf below,
While he stood all unscathed, safe from the overthrow.

'Stood,' said I? Nay, in wonder and in love
As on that more than vision Godfrey gazed,
He fell at his Deliverer's feet, and praised
With a new sweetness, sweet as harps above,
The glorious One, whose royal grace had saved
The aimless wanderer, who never grace had craved.

Far in the night this wondrous watch he kept
With the unslumbering Shepherd, while a joy,
The first he ever knew without alloy,
Filled all his soul with light. At last he slept,
Wrapped in this strange new peace, whose steady beam
Made all his past life seem a sinful, troubled dream.

What then? It was no zenith, though the star
Of life shone out at radiant height, that dimmed
Each previous gleam to gloom that barely rimmed
The shifting clouds, with something, that, from far
Might have been fancied light, yet only made
The darkness more discerned, the spirit more afraid.

Rather, it was the rising! the first hour
Of the true shining, that should rise and rise
From glory unto glory, through God's skies,
In strengthening brightness and increasing power.
A rising with no setting, for its height
Could only culminate in God's eternal light.

The feeble glimmer of the former days,
The hope, the love, the very glee, that paled
Just at their seeming zenith, and then failed
Of fuller sparkling,—all the scattered rays
Were caught up and transfigured, in the blaze
Of the new life of love, and energy, and praise.

The joy of loyal service to the King
Shone through them all, and lit up other lives
With the new fire of faith, that ever strives,
Like a swift-kindling beacon, far to fling

The tidings of His victory, and claim
New subjects for His realm, new honour for His Name.

And so the years flowed on, and only cast
Light, and more light, upon the shining way,
That more and more shone to the perfect day;
Always intenser, clearer than the past;
Because they only bore him on glad wing
Nearer the Light of Light, the Presence of the King.

Who recks the short recession of a wave
In the strong flowing of a tide? And so
Without a pang could Godfrey leave below
Successive earthly zeniths, while he gave
A glad glance upward to the rainbow Throne,
And joyously pressed on to nobler heights alone.

Or if awhile a looming sorrow-cloud
He entered, still he found the Glory there,
Shechinah-brightness resting still and fair
Within the holy curtains, as he bowed
Before the Presence on the Mercy-seat;
Then forth he came with sound of golden bells most sweet.

And then the music floated on the wind,
A constant carol of glad tidings told,
Of how the lives the One Life doth enfold
Are ever with that Life so closely twined,
That nought can separate, below, above,
And life itself is one long miracle of love.

At last the gentle tone was heard, that falls
In all-mysterious sweetness on the ear
That long has listened, longing, without fear,
Because so well it knows the Voice that calls;
Though only once that solemn call is heard,
While angel-songs take up the echoes of the word.

'Friend, go up higher!' So he took that night
The one grand step, beyond the stars of God,

Into the splendour, shadowless and broad,
Into the everlasting joy and light.
The Zenith of the earthly life was come;
What marvel that the lips were for the moment dumb!

What then? Eye hath not seen, ear hath not heard!
Wait till thou too hast fought the noble strife,
And won, through Jesus Christ, the crown of life!
Then shalt thou know the glory of the word,
Then as the stars for ever—ever shine,
Beneath the King's own smile,—perpetual Zenith thine!

The Ministry of Intercession.

THERE is no holy service
But hath its secret bliss:
Yet, of all blessèd ministries,
Is one so dear as this?
The ministry that cannot be
A wondering seraph's dower,
Enduing mortal weakness
With more than angel-power,
The ministry of purest love
Uncrossed by any fear,
That bids us meet at the Master's feet,
And keeps us very near.

God's ministers are many,
For this His gracious will,
Remembrancers that day and night
This holy office fill.
While some are hushed in slumber,
Some to fresh service wake,
And thus the saintly number
No change or chance can break.
And thus the sacred courses
Are evermore fulfilled,
The tide of grace by time or place
Is never stayed or stilled.

Oh, if our ears were opened
  To hear as angels do
The Intercession-chorus
  Arising full and true,
We should hear it soft up-welling
  In morning's pearly light,
Through evening's shadows swelling
  In grandly gathering might,
The sultry silence filling
  Of noontide's thunderous glow,
And the solemn starlight thrilling
  With ever deepening flow.

We should hear it through the rushing
  Of the city's restless roar,
And trace its gentle gushing
  O'er ocean's crystal floor:
We should hear it far up-floating
  Beneath the Orient moon,
And catch the golden noting
  From the busy Western noon,
And pine-robed heights would echo
  As the mystic chant up-floats,
And the sunny plain resound again
  With the myriad-mingling notes.

Who are the blessèd ministers
  Of this world-gathering band?
All who have learnt One Language,
  Through each far-parted land;
All who have learnt the story
  Of Jesu's love and grace,
And are longing for His glory
  To shine in every face.
All who have known the Father
  In Jesus Christ our Lord,
And know the might and love the light
  Of the Spirit in the Word.

Yet there are some who see not
  Their calling high and grand,

Who seldom pass the portals,
    And never boldly stand
Before the golden altar
    On the crimson-stainèd floor,
Who wait afar and falter,
    And dare not hope for more.
Will ye not join the blessèd ranks
    In their beautiful array?
Let intercession blend with thanks
    As ye minister to-day!

There are little ones among them,
    Child-ministers of prayer,
White robes of intercession
    Those tiny servants wear.
First for the near and dear ones
    Is that fair ministry,
Then for the poor black children,
    So far beyond the sea.
The busy hands are folded,
    As the little heart uplifts
In simple love, to God above,
    Its prayer for all good gifts.

There are hands too often weary
    With the business of the day,
With God-entrusted duties,
    Who are toiling while they pray,
They bear the golden vials,
    And the golden harps of praise,
Through all the daily trials,
    Through all the dusty ways.
These hands, so tired, so faithful,
    With odours sweet are filled,
And in the ministry of prayer
    Are wonderfully skilled.

There are ministers unlettered,
    Not of Earth's great and wise,
Yet mighty and unfettered
    Their eagle-prayers arise.

Free of the heavenly storehouse!
They hold the master-key
That opens all the fulness
Of God's great treasury.
They bring the needs of others,
And all things are their own,
For their one grand claim is Jesu's name
Before their Father's throne.

There are noble Christian workers,
The men of faith and power,
The overcoming wrestlers
Of many a midnight hour;
Prevailing princes with their God,
Who will not be denied,
Who bring down showers of blessing
To swell the rising tide.
The Prince of Darkness quaileth
At their triumphant way,
Their fervent prayer availeth
To sap his subtle sway.

But in this Temple-service
Are sealed and set apart
Arch-priests of intercession,
Of undivided heart.
The fulness of anointing
On these is doubly shed,
The consecration of their God
Is on each low-bowed head.
They bear the golden vials
With white and trembling hand
In quiet room or wakeful gloom
These ministers must stand,—

To the Intercession-Priesthood
Mysteriously ordained,
When the strange dark gift of suffering
This added gift hath gained.
For the holy hands uplifted
In suffering's longest hour

Are truly Spirit-gifted
　With intercession-power.
The Lord of Blessing fills them
　With His uncounted gold,
An unseen store, still more and more,
　Those trembling hands shall hold.

Not always with rejoicing
　This ministry is wrought,
For many a sigh is mingled
　With the sweet odours brought.
Yet every tear bedewing
　The faith-fed altar fire
May be its bright renewing
　To purer flame, and higher.
But when the oil of gladness
　God graciously outpours,
The heavenward blaze with blended praise
　More mightily upsoars.

So the incense-cloud ascendeth
　As through calm crystal air,
A pillar reaching unto heaven,
　Of wreathèd faith and prayer.
For evermore the Angel
　Of Intercession stands
In His Divine High Priesthood,
　With fragrance-fillèd hands,
To wave the golden censer
　Before His Father's throne,
With Spirit-fire intenser,
　And incense all His own.

And evermore the Father
　Sends radiantly down
All-marvellous responses,
　His ministers to crown;
The incense-cloud returning
　As golden blessing-showers,

We in each drop discerning
  Some feeble prayer of ours,
Transmuted into wealth unpriced,
  By Him who giveth thus
The glory all to Jesus Christ,
  The gladness all to us!

The Voice of Many Waters.

Far away I heard it,
  Stealing through the pines,
Like a whisper saintly,
Falling dimly, faintly,
  Through the terraced vines.

Freshening breezes bore it
  Down the mountain slope;
So I turned and listened,
While the sunlight glistened
  On the snowy cope.

Far away and dreamy
  Was the Voice I heard;
Yet it pierced and found me,
Through the voices round me—
  Song without a word.

All the life and turmoil,
  All the busy cheer
Melted in the flowing
Of that murmur, growing,
  Claiming all my ear.

What the mountain-message,
  I could never tell;
Such Æolian fluting
Hath no language suiting
  What we write and spell.

Rather did it enter
    Where no words can win,
Touching and unsealing
Springs of hidden feeling,
    Slumbering deep within.

Voice of many waters
    Only heard afar!
Hushing, luring slowly,
With an influence holy,
    Like the Orient Star.

Follow where it leadeth,
    Till we stand below,
While the noble thunder
Wins the hush of wonder,
    Silent in its glow.

Light and sound triumphant
    Fill the eye and ear;
Every pulse is beating
Quick unconscious greeting
    To the vision near.

Rainbow-flames are wreathing
    In the dazzling foam,
Fancy far transcending,
Power and beauty blending
    In their radiant home.

All the dreamy longing
    Passes out of sight,
In a swift surrender
To the joyous splendour
    Of this song of might.

Self is lost and hidden
    As it peals along;

Fevered introspection,
Paler-browed reflection
    Vanish in the song.

For the spirit, lifted
    From the dulling mists,
Takes a stronger moulding,
As the sound enfolding,
    Bears it where it lists.

Voice of many waters!
    Must we turn away
From the crystal chorus
Now resounding o'er us
    Through the flashing spray!

Far away we hear it,
    Floating from the sky;
Mystic echo, falling
Through the stars, and calling
    From the thrones on high.

There are voices round us,
    Busy, quick, and loud;
All day long we hear them,
We are still so near them,
    Still among the crowd.

Yet athwart the clamour
    Falls it, faint and sweet,
Like the softest harp-tone,
Passing every sharp tone
    Down the noisy street.

To the soul-recesses
    Cleaving then its way,
Waking hidden yearning,
Unwilled impulse turning
    To the Far Away.

Far away—and viewless,
    Yet not all unknown—

In the murmur tracing
Soft notes interlacing
    With familiar tone.

So we start and listen!
    While the murmur low
Falleth ever clearer,
Swelleth fuller, nearer
    In melodious flow.

Voice of many waters
    From the height above
Hushing, luring slowly
With its influence holy,
    With its song of love!

Following where it leadeth,
    Pilgrim feet shall stand,
Where the holy millions
Throng the fair pavilions
    In the Glorious Land.

Where the sevenfold 'Worthy!'
    Hails the King of kings,
Blent with golden clashing
Of the crowns, and flashing
    Of cherubic wings;

Rolls the Amen Chorus,
    Old, yet ever new;
Seal of blest allegiance,
Pledge of bright obedience,
    Seal that God is true.

Through the solemn glory
    Alleluias rise,
Mightiest exultation,
Holiest adoration,
    Infinite surprise.

There immortal powers
    Meet immortal song,
Heavenly image bearing,
Angel-essence sharing,
    Excellent and strong.

Strong to bear the glory
    And the veil-less sight,
Strong to swell the thunders
And to know the wonders
    Of the home of light.

Voice of many waters!
    Everlasting laud!
Hark! it rushes nearer,
Every moment clearer,
    From the Throne of God!

'Free to Serve.'

SHE chose His service. For the Lord of Love
Had chosen her, and paid the awful price
For her redemption; and had sought her out,
And set her free, and clothed her gloriously,
And put His royal ring upon her hand,
And crowns of loving-kindness on her head.
She chose it. Yet it seemed she could not yield
The fuller measure other lives could bring;
For He had given her a precious gift,
A treasure and a charge to prize and keep,
A tiny hand, a darling hand, that traced
On her heart's tablet words of golden love.
And there was not much room for other lines,
For time and thought were spent (and rightly spent,
For He had given the charge), and hours and days
Were concentrated on the one dear task.

But He had need of her. Not one new gem,
But many, for His crown;—not one fair sheaf,

But many, she should bring. And she should have
A richer, happier harvest-home at last,
Because more fruit, more glory, and more praise,
Her life should yield to Him. And so He came,
The Master came Himself, and gently took
The little hand in His, and gave it room
Among the angel-harpers. Jesus came
And laid His own hand on the quivering heart,
And made it very still, that He might write
Invisible words of power—'Free to serve!'
Then through the darkness and the chill He sent
A heat-ray of His love, developing
The mystic writing, till it glowed and shone
And lit up all her life with radiance new,—
The happy service of a yielded heart.
With comfort that He never ceased to give,
Because her need could never cease, she filled
The empty chalices of other lives,
And time and thought were thenceforth spent for Him
Who loved her with His everlasting love.

Let Him write what He will upon our hearts
With His unerring pen. They are His Own,
Hewn from the rock by His selecting grace,
Prepared for His own glory. Let Him write!
Be sure He will not cross out one sweet word
But to inscribe a sweeter,—but to grave
One that shall shine for ever to His praise,
And thus fulfil our deepest heart-desire.
The tearful eye at first may read the line
'Bondage to grief!' but He shall wipe away
The tears, and clear the vision, till it read
In ever-brightening letters, 'Free to serve!'
For whom the Son makes free is free indeed.

Nor only by reclaiming His good gifts,
But by withholding, doth the Master write
These words upon the heart. Not always needs
Erasure of some blessèd line of love

For this more blest inscription. Where He finds
A tablet empty for the ' lines left out,'
That ' might have been ' engraved with human love
And sweetest human cares, yet never bore
That poetry of life, His own dear hand
Writes ' Free to serve!' And these clear characters
Fill with fair colours all the unclaimed space,
Else grey and colourless.
Then let it be
The motto of our lives until we stand
In the great freedom of Eternity,
Where we '*shall* serve Him' while we see His face,
For ever and for ever ' Free to serve.'

Coming to the King.

2 Chronicles 9:1–12.

I came from very far away to see
The King of Salem; for I had been told
Of glory and of wisdom manifold,
And condescension infinite and free.
How could I rest, when I had heard His fame,
In that dark lonely land of death from whence I came?

I came (but not like Sheba's Queen), alone!
No stately train, no costly gifts to bring;
No friend at court, save One, that One the King!
I had requests to spread before His throne,
And I had questions none could solve for me,
Of import deep, and full of awful mystery.

I came and communed with that mighty King,
And told Him all my heart; I cannot say,
In mortal ear, what communings were they.
But wouldst thou know, go too, and meekly bring
All that is in thy heart, and thou shalt hear
His voice of love and power, His answers sweet and clear.

O happy end of every weary quest!
He told me all I needed, graciously;—

Enough for guidance, and for victory
O'er doubts and fears, enough for quiet rest;
And when some veiled response I could not read,
It was not hid from Him,—this was enough indeed.

His wisdom and His glories passed before
My wondering eyes in gradual revelation;
The house that He had built, its strong foundation,
Its living stones; and, brightening more and more,
Fair glimpses of that palace far away,
Where all His loyal ones shall dwell with Him for aye.

True the report that reached my far-off land
Of all His wisdom and transcendent fame;
Yet I believèd not until I came,—
Bowed to the dust till raised by royal hand.
The half was never told by mortal word;
My King exceeded all the fame that I had heard!

Oh, happy are His servants! happy they
Who stand continually before His face,
Ready to do His will of wisest grace!
My King! is mine such blessedness to-day?
For I too hear Thy wisdom, line by line,
Thy ever-brightening words in holy radiance shine.

Oh, blessèd be the Lord thy God! who set
Our King upon His throne. Divine delight
In the Belovèd crowning Thee with might,
Honour, and majesty supreme; and yet
The strange and Godlike secret opening thus,—
The kingship of His Christ ordained through love to us!

What shall I render to my glorious King?
I have but that which I receive from Thee;
And what I give, Thou givest back to me,
Transmuted by Thy touch; each worthless thing
Changed to the preciousness of gem or gold,
And by Thy blessing multiplied a thousand-fold.

All my desire Thou grantest, whatsoe'er
I ask! Was ever mythic tale or dream
So bold as this reality,—this stream
Of boundless blessings flowing full and free?
Yet more than I have thought or asked of Thee,
Out of Thy royal bounty still Thou givest me.

Now I will turn to my own land, and tell
What I myself have seen and heard of Thee,
And give Thine own sweet message, 'Come and see!'
And yet in heart and mind for ever dwell
With Thee, my King of Peace, in loyal rest,
Within the fair pavilion of Thy presence blest.

'Surely in what place my Lord the King shall be, whether in death or life, even there also will thy servant be.'—2 Samuel 15:21.

'Where I am, there shall also My servant be.'—John 12:26.

Far More Exceeding.

καθ' ὑπερβολὴν εἰς ὑπερβολὴν.—2 Corinthians 4:17.

'From glory unto glory!' Thank God, that even here
The starry words are shining out, our heavenward way to cheer!
That e'en among the shadows the conquering brightness glows,
As ever from the nearing Light intenser radiance flows.

'From glory unto glory!' Shall the grand progression fail
When the darkening glass is shattered as we pass within the veil?
Shall the joyous song of 'Onward!' at once for ever cease,
And the swelling music culminate in monotone of peace?

Shall the fuller life be sundered at the portal of its bliss,
From the principle of growth entwined with every nerve of this?
Shall the holy law of progress be hopelessly repealed,
And the moment of releasing see our sum of glory sealed?

The tender touch of moonlight, with an orbit quickly run,
The lustre of the planet, circling slowly round the sun,
The mighty revolutions of its million-heated blaze,
'From glory unto glory' lead our far-expanding gaze.

Then onward, ever onward, through the unexplored abyss
(Dark barrier between the suns of other worlds and this),
Until the measure-unit mocks the grasp of human thought,
And space and time commingle while the clue is feebly sought.

Till, in that wider ocean, deep calleth unto deep,
Star-glories with attendant worlds, forth-flashing as they sweep
Around their unseen centre, that point of mystic power,
In unimagined cycles, where an age is but an hour.

Then! onward and yet onward! for the dim revealings show
That systems unto systems in grand succession grow,
That what we deemed a volume but one golden verse may be,
One rhythmic cadence in the flow of God's great poetry.

That what we deemed a symphony was one all-thrilling bar,
Through aisles of His great temple resounding full and far;
That what we deemed an ocean was a shallow by the shore!
Then! onward yet, in eagle flight, through the Infinite we soar—

'From glory unto glory,' till the spirit fails; and then
Illimitable vistas still opening to our ken,
Mysterious immensities of order and of light,
Stretch far beyond our farthest thought, as thought beyond our sight.

But the starting-point in heaven shall be no 'glory of the moon,'
No planet gleam, no stellar fire, no blaze of tropic noon;
From 'glory that excelleth' all that human heart hath known,
Our 'onward, upward,' shall begin in the presence of the Throne.

'From glory unto glory' of loveliness and light,
Of music and of rapture, of power and of sight,
'From glory unto glory' of knowledge and of love,
Shall be the joy of progress awaiting us above.

'From glory unto glory' that ever lies before,
Still wondering, adoring, rejoicing more and more,
Still following where He leadeth, from shining field to field,
Himself the goal of glory, Revealer and Revealed!

'From glory unto glory' with no limit and no veil,
With wings that cannot weary and hearts that cannot fail;

Within, without, no hindrance, no barrier as we soar;
And never interruption to the endless 'more and more'!

For infinite outpourings of Jehovah's love and grace,
And infinite unveilings of the brightness of His face,
And infinite unfoldings of the splendour of His will,
Meet the mightiest expansions of the finite spirit still.

O Saviour, hast Thou ransomed us from death's unknown abyss,
And purchased with Thy precious blood such everlasting bliss?
Art Thou indeed preparing us, with love exceeding great,
And preparing all this glory in such 'far exceeding weight'?

Then let our hearts be surely fixed where truest joys are found,
And let our burning, loving praise, yet more and more abound;
And, gazing on the 'things not seen,' eternal in the skies,
'From glory unto glory,' O Saviour, let us rise!

'The Splendour of God's Will.'

In the freshness of the spring-time,
In the beauty of the May,
When the swift-winged breezes carolled,
And the lambs were all at play,
And the birds were blithe and busy,
Upon her couch she lay.

Like a lily bruised and drooping,
Before its early flower
Had fully opened to the sun,
Or reached a noontide hour:
Broken and yet more fragrant
For the heavy-beating shower.

It was not the first spring-time
Passed without one glad sight
Of a starry primrose growing,
Or a brooklet swift and bright,

And without one bounding footstep
    On a field with daisies white.

It was not the first spring-time—
    And it might not be the last
In weariness and suffering
    Thus to be slowly passed;
For when the young feet cannot move
    Months do not travel fast.

And yet she saw what others
    Have never sought or seen,
A splendour more than spring-light
    On fair trees waving green,
And more than summer sunshine
    On Ocean's silver sheen.

Her pencil, tracing feebly
    Words that shall echo still,
Perchance some unknown mission
    May joyously fulfil:—
'I think I just begin to see
    The *splendour* of God's will!'

O words of golden music
    Caught from the harps on high,
Which find a glorious anthem
    Where we have found a sigh,
And peal their grandest praises
    Just where ours faint and die!

O words of holy radiance
    Shining on every tear,
Till it becomes a rainbow,
    Reflecting, bright and clear,
Our Father's love and glory
    So wonderful, so dear!

O words of sparkling power,
    Of insight full and deep!

Shall they not enter other hearts
  In a grand and gladsome sweep,
And lift the lives to songs of joy
  That only droop and weep?

For her, God's will was suffering,
  Just waiting, lying still!
Days passing on in weariness,
  In shadows deep and chill;
And yet she had begun to see
  The Splendour of God's Will!

And oh, it is a splendour,
  A glow of majesty,
A mystery of beauty,
  If we will only see;
A very cloud of glory
  Enfolding you and me.

A splendour that is lighted
  At one transcendent flame,
The wondrous Love, the perfect Love,
  Our Father's sweetest name;
For His very Name, and Essence,
  And His Will are all the same!

A splendour that is shining
  Upon His children's way;
That guides the willing footsteps
  That do not want to stray,
And that leads them ever onward
  Unto the perfect day.

A splendour that illumines,
  Th' abysses of the Past
And marvels of the Future,
  Sublime and bright and vast;
While o'er our tiny Present
  A flood of light is cast.

No twilight falls upon it,
    No shadow dims its ray,
No darkness overcomes it,
    No night can end its day;
It hath unending triumph
    And everlasting sway.

Blest Will of God! most glorious,
    The very fount of grace,
Whence all the goodness floweth
    That heart can ever trace—
Temple whose pinnacles are love,
    And faithfulness its base.

Blest Will of God! whose splendour
    Is dawning on the world,
On hearts in which Christ's banner
    Is manfully unfurled,
On hearts of childlike meekness,
    With dew of youth impearled.

O Spirit of Jehovah,
    Reveal this glory still!
That many an empty chalice
    Sweet thanks and praise may fill,
When, like this 'little one,' they see
    'The Splendour of God's Will':

That faith may win the vision
    That hers hath early won,
And gaze upon the splendour,
    And own the cloudless sun,
And join the seraph song of love,
    And *sing*—'Thy Will be done!'

The Two Paths.

VIA DOLOROSA AND VIA GIOJOSA.

(*Suggested by a Picture.*)

My Master, they have wronged Thee and Thy love!
They only told me I should find the path
A Via Dolorosa all the way!
Even Thy sweetest singers only sang
Of pressing onward through the same sharp thorns,
With bleeding footsteps, through the chill dark mist,
Following and struggling till they reach the light,
The rest, the sunshine of the far beyond.
The anthems of the pilgrimage were set
In most pathetic minors, exquisite,
Yet breathing sadness more than any praise.
Thy minstrels let the fitful breezes make
Æolian moans on their entrusted harps,
Until the listeners thought that this was all
The music Thou hadst given. And so the steps
That halted where the two ways met and crossed,
The broad and narrow, turned aside in fear,
Thinking the radiance of their youth must pass
In sombre shadows if they followed Thee;
Hearing afar such echoes of one strain,
The cross, the tribulation, and the toil,
The conflict, and the clinging in the dark.
What wonder that the dancing feet are stayed
From entering the only path of peace!
Master, forgive them! Tune their harps anew,
And put a new song in their mouths for Thee,
And make Thy chosen people joyful in Thy love.
    Lord Jesus, Thou hast trodden once for all
The Via Dolorosa,—and for *us!*
No artist-power or minstrel-gift may tell
The cost to Thee of each unfaltering step,
Where love that passeth knowledge led Thee on,
Faithful and true to God, and true to us.
    And now, belovèd Lord, Thou callest us

To follow Thee, and we will take Thy word
About the path which Thou hast marked for us.
Narrow indeed it is! Who does not choose
The narrow track upon the mountain-side,
With ever-widening view, and freshening air,
And honeyed heather, rather than the road,
With smoothest breadth of dust and loss of view,
Soiled blossoms not worth gathering, and the noise
Of wheels instead of silence of the hills,
Or music of the waterfalls? Oh, why
Should they misrepresent Thy words, and make
'Narrow' synonymous with 'very hard'?
For Thou, Divinest Wisdom, Thou hast said
Thy ways are ways of pleasantness, and all
Thy paths are peace; and that the path of him
Who wears Thy perfect robe of righteousness,
Is as the light that shineth more and more
Unto the perfect day. And Thou hast given
An olden promise, rarely quoted now,[1]
Because it is too bright for our weak faith:
'If they obey and serve Him, they shall spend
Days in prosperity, and they shall spend
Their years in pleasures.' All because *Thy* days
Were full of sorrow, and Thy lonely years
Were passed in grief's acquaintance—all for us!
Master, I set my seal that Thou art true!
Of Thy good promise not one thing hath failed,
And I would send a ringing challenge forth,
To all who know Thy name, to tell it out,
Thy faithfulness to every written word,
Thy loving-kindness crowning all the days,—
To say and sing with me: 'The Lord is good,
His mercy is for ever, and His truth
Is written on each page of all my life!'
Yes! there *is* tribulation, but Thy power
Can blend it with rejoicing. There *are* thorns,
But they have kept us in the narrow way,
The King's highway of holiness and peace.
And there *is* chastening, but the Father's love

[1] Job 26:9

Flows through it; and would any trusting heart
Forego the chastening and forego the love?
And every step leads on to 'more and more,'—
From strength to strength Thy pilgrims pass, and sing
The praise of Him who leads them on and on,
From glory unto glory, even here!

'Vessels of Mercy, Prepared unto Glory.'

Romans 9:23.

Vessels of mercy, prepared unto glory!
  This is your calling and this is your joy!
This, for the new year unfolding before ye,
  Tells out the terms of your blessèd employ.

Vessels, it may be, all empty and broken,
  Marred in the Hand of inscrutable skill;
(Love can accept the mysterious token!)
  Marred but to make them more beautiful still

Jeremiah 18:4.

Vessels, it may be, not costly or golden;
  Vessels, it may be, of quantity small,
Yet by the Nail in the Sure Place upholden,
  Never to shiver and never to fall.

Isaiah 22:23, 24.

Vessels to honour, made sacred and holy,
  Meet for the use of the Master we love,
Ready for service all simple and lowly,
  Ready, one day, for the temple above.

2 Timothy 2:21.

Yes, though the vessels be fragile and earthen,
  God hath commanded His glory to shine;
Treasure resplendent henceforth is our burthen,
  Excellent power, not ours but Divine.

2 Corinthians 4:5, 6.

Chosen in Christ ere the dawn of Creation,
Chosen for Him, to be filled with His grace,
Chosen to carry the streams of salvation
Into each thirsty and desolate place.

Acts 9:15.

Take all Thy vessels, O glorious Finer,
Purge all the dross, that each chalice may be
Pure in Thy pattern, completer, diviner,
Filled with Thy glory and shining for Thee.

Proverbs 25:4.

Only for Jesus.

Only for Jesus! Lord, keep it for ever
Sealed on the heart and engraved on the life!
Pulse of all gladness and nerve of endeavour,
Secret of rest, and the strength of our strife.

'Daily Afterwards.'

(From F. R. H. to K. T.)

'There is no "afterward" on earth for me!'
Beloved, 'tis not so!
That God's own 'afterwards' are pledged to thee,
Thy life shall show.

No 'afterward' indeed of great things wrought,
By willing hands and feet;
No sheaf is thine, from wider harvests brought,
With singing sweet.

Fair flowing years of ease and laughing strength,
With cloudless morning skies,
Sweet life renewed, and active work at length,
His love denies.

But living fruit of righteousness to Him
    His chastening shall yield,
And constant 'afterwards,' no longer dim,
    Shall be revealed.

Is it no 'afterward' that in thy heart
    His *love* is shed abroad?
And that His Spirit breathes, while called apart,
    The *peace* of God?

That *joy* in tribulation shall spring forth
    To greet His visits blessed,
Whose wisdom wakes the south wind or the north,
    As He sees best!

Shall not *longsuffering* in thee be wrought,
    To mirror back His own?
His *gentleness* shall mellow every thought,
    And look, and tone.

And *goodness!* In thyself dwells no good thing,
    Yet from thy glorious Root
An 'afterward' of holiness shall spring—
    Most precious fruit!

The trial of thy *faith* from hour to hour
    Shall yield a grand increase;
He shall fulfil the work of faith with power
    That cannot cease.

And all around shall praise Him as they see
    The *meekness* of thy Lord.
Thus, even here and now, how blest shall be
    Thy sure reward!

This pleasant fruit it shall be thine to lay
    At thy Belovèd's feet,
The ripening clusters growing day by day
    More full and sweet.

If at His gate He keeps thee waiting now
    Through many a suffering year,

Watch for His daily 'afterwards,' and thou
Shalt find them here:

Till, as refinèd gold, in thee shall shine
His image, no more dim;
Then shall the endless 'afterward' be thine
Of rest with Him.

Sunday Night.

Rest him, O Father! Thou didst send him forth
With great and gracious messages of love;
But Thy ambassador is weary now,
Worn with the weight of his high embassy.
Now care for him as Thou hast cared for us
In sending him; and cause him to lie down
In Thy fresh pastures, by Thy streams of peace.
Let Thy left hand be now beneath his head,
And Thine upholding right encircle him,
And, underneath, the Everlasting arms
Be felt in full support. So let him rest,
Hushed like a little child, without one care,
And so give Thy belovèd sleep to-night.

Rest him, dear Master! He hath poured for us
The wine of joy, and we have been refreshed.
Now fill *his* chalice, give him sweet new draughts
Of life and love, with Thine own hand; be Thou
His ministrant to-night; draw very near
In all Thy tenderness and all Thy power.
Oh speak to him! Thou knowest how to speak
A word in season to Thy weary ones,
And he is weary now. Thou lovest him—
Let Thy disciple lean upon Thy breast,
And, leaning, gain new strength to 'rise and shine.'

Rest him, O loving Spirit! Let Thy calm
Fall on his soul to-night. O holy Dove,
Spread Thy bright wing above him, let him rest
Beneath its shadow; let him know afresh

The infinite truth and might of Thy dear name—
'Our Comforter!' As gentlest touch will stay
The strong vibrations of a jarring chord,
So lay Thy hand upon his heart, and still
Each overstraining throb, each pulsing pain.
Then, in the stillness, breathe upon the strings,
And let Thy holy music overflow
With soothing power his listening, resting soul.

Memorial Names.

The High Priest stands before the Mercy Seat,
And on his breast bright mingling jewel-flames
Reflect Shechinah light; twelve patriarch names
Flash where the emerald and sapphire meet
Sardius and diamond. With softer beam,
From mystic onyx on his shoulders placed,
Deep graven, never altered or erased,
The same great names, in birthday order, gleam.
May each name written here be thus engraved,
Set in the place of power, the place of love,
And borne in sweet memorial above,
By Him who loved and chose, redeemed and saved
Be each dear name, the greatest and the least,
Always upon the heart of our High Priest.

Precious Things.

I.

Oh what shining revelation of His treasures God hath given!
Precious things of grace and glory, precious things of earth and heaven.
Holy Spirit, now unlock them with Thy mighty golden key,
Royal jewels of the kingdom let us now adoring see!

II.

'Unto you therefore which believe, He is precious,'—1 Peter 2:7.

Christ is precious, oh most precious, gift by God the Father sealed;
Pearl of greatest price and treasure, hidden, yet to us revealed;
His own people's crown of glory, and resplendent diadem;
More than thousand worlds, and dearer than all life and love to them.

III.

'Behold, I lay in Zion a chief comer stone, elect, precious.'—1 Peter 2:6.

Marvellous and very precious is the Corner Stone Elect;
Though rejected by the builders, chosen by the Architect;
All-supporting, all-uniting, and all-crowning, tried and sure;
True Foundation, yet true Headstone of His temple bright and pure.

IV.

'Ye know that ye were not redeemed with corruptible things, . . . but with the precious blood of Christ, as of a lamb without blemish and without spot.'—1 Peter 1:18, 19.

Now, in reverent love and wonder, touch the theme of deepest laud,
Precious blood of Christ that bought us and hath made us nigh to God!
His own blood, O love unfathomed! shed for those who loved Him not;
Mighty fountain always open, cleansing us from every spot.

V.

'How precious also are Thy thoughts unto me, O God! how great is the sum of them!'
—Psalm 139:17.

Oh, how wonderful and precious are Thy thoughts to us, O God!
Outlined in Creation, blazoned on Redemption's banner broad;

Infinite and deep and dazzling as the noontide heavens above;
Yet *more* wonderful to usward are Thy thoughts of peace and love.

VI.

'Whereby are given unto us exceeding great and precious promises, that by these ye might be partakers of the divine nature.'—2 PETER 1:4.

Then, exceeding great and precious are Thy promises Divine;
Given by Christ, and by the Spirit sealed with sweetest 'All are thine!'
Precious in their peace and power, in their sure and changeless might,
Strengthening, comforting, transforming; suns by day and stars by night.

VII.

'To them that have obtained like precious faith with us through the righteousness of God, and our Saviour Jesus Christ.'—2 PETER 1:1.

Precious faith our God hath given; rich in faith is rich indeed!
Fire-tried gold from His own treasury, fully meeting every need:
Channel of His grace abounding; bringing peace and joy and light;
Purifying, overcoming; linking weakness with His might.

VIII.

'The precious ointment upon the head, that ran down upon the beard, even Aaron's beard; that went down to the skirts of his garments.'—PSALM 133:2.

Precious ointment, very costly, of chief odours pure and sweet,
Holy gift for royal priesthood, thus for temple-service meet;
Such the Spirit's precious unction, oil of gladness freely shed,
Sanctifying and abiding on the consecrated head.

IX.

'How excellent (*marg.* precious) is Thy loving kindness, O God! therefore the children of men put their trust under the shadow of Thy wings.'—PSALM 36:7; ISAIAH 54:8, 10.

Who shall paint the flash of splendour from the opened casket bright,
When His precious loving-kindness beams upon the quickened sight!
Priceless jewel ever gleaming with imperishable ray,
God will never take it from us, though the mountains pass away.

X.

'It cannot be valued with the gold of Ophir, with the precious onyx, or the sapphire. No mention shall be made of coral or of pearls: for the price of wisdom is above rubies.'—Job 28:16, 18.

Far more precious than the ruby, or the crystal's rainbow light,
Valued not with precious onyx or with pearl and sapphire bright,
Freely given to all who ask it, is the wisdom from above,
Pure and peaceable and gentle, full of fruits of life and love.

XI.

'Blessed of the Lord be his land for the precious things of heaven, for the dew, and for the deep that coucheth beneath, and for the precious fruits brought forth by the sun, and for the precious things put forth by the moon, and for the chief things of the ancient mountains, and for the precious things of the lasting hills, and for the precious things of the earth.'—Deuteronomy 33.13–16.

Nor withhold we glad thanksgiving for His mercies ever new,
Precious things of earth and heaven, sun and rain and quickening dew;
Precious fruits and varied crowning of the year His goodness fills,
Chief things of the ancient mountains, precious things of lasting hills.

XII.

'If thou take forth the precious from the vile, thou shalt be as My mouth.'
—Jeremiah 15:19.

Such His gifts! but mark we duly our responsibility
Unto Him whose name is Holy, infinite in purity;
Sin and self no longer serving, take the precious from the vile,
So His power shall rest upon thee, thou shalt dwell beneath His smile.

XIII.

'The precious sons of Zion, comparable to fine gold.'—Lamentations 4:2.

Sons of Zion, ye are precious in your heavenly Father's sight,
Ye are His peculiar treasure, ye His jewels of delight;
Sought and chosen, cleansed and polished, purchased with
transcendent cost,
Kept in His own royal casket, never, never to be lost.

XIV.

'That the trial of your faith, being much more precious than of gold that perisheth, though it be tried with fire, might be found unto praise and honour and glory at the appearing of Jesus Christ.'—1 PETER 1:7.

Precious, more than gold that wasteth, is the trial of your faith,
Fires of anguish or temptation cannot dim it, cannot scathe!
Your Refiner sitteth watching till His image shineth clear,
For His glory, praise, and honour, when the Saviour shall appear.

XV.

'Precious in the sight of the Lord is the death of His saints.'—PSALM 116:15.

Precious, precious to Jehovah is His children's holy sleep;
He is with them in the passing through the waters cold and deep;
Everlasting love enfolds them softly, safely to His breast,
Everlasting love receives them to His glory and His rest.

XVI.

'He showed me that great city, the holy Jerusalem, descending out of heaven from God, having the glory of God: and her light was like unto a stone most precious; even like a jasper stone, clear as crystal.'—REVELATION 21:10, 11.

Pause not here,—the Holy City, glorious in God's light, behold!
Like unto a stone most precious, clear as crystal, pure as gold;
Strong foundations, fair with sapphires, sardius and chrysolite,
Blent with amethyst and jacinth, emerald and topaz bright.

XVII.

'A city which hath foundations, whose builder and maker is God.'—HEBREWS 11:10.

Glorious dwelling of the holy, where no grief or gloom of sin
Through the pure and pearly portals evermore shall enter in:
Christ its Light and God its Temple, Christ its song of endless laud!
Oh what precious consummation of the precious things of God!

Tiny Tokens.

I.

The murmur of a waterfall
A mile away,
The rustle when a robin lights
Upon a spray,
The lapping of a lowland stream
On dipping boughs,
The sound of grazing from a herd
Of gentle cows,
The echo from a wooded hill
Of cuckoo's call,
The quiver through the meadow grass
At evening fall:—
Too subtle are these harmonies
For pen and rule,
Such music is not understood
By any school:
But when the brain is overwrought,
It hath a spell,
Beyond all human skill and power,
To make it well.

II.

The memory of a kindly word
For long gone by,
The fragrance of a fading flower
Sent lovingly,
The gleaming of a sudden smile
Or sudden tear,
The warmer pressure of the hand,
The tone of cheer,
The hush that means 'I cannot speak,
But I have heard!'
The note that only bears a verse
From God's own Word:—

Such tiny things we hardly count
As ministry;
The givers deeming they have shown
Scant sympathy:
But when the heart is overwrought,
Oh, who can tell
The power of such tiny things
To make it well!

Mischief Making.

I.

Only a tiny dropping
From a tiny hidden leak;
But the flow is never stopping,
And the flaw is far to seek.

Only some trickling water,
Nothing at all at first;
But it grows to a valley-slaughter,
For the reservoir has burst!

The wild flood once in motion,
Who shall arrest its course?
As well restrain the ocean
As that ungoverned force!

Mourn for the desolations,
And help the ruined men,
Till next spring's fair creations
Make the valley smile again.

Help with a free, pure pity,
For your hands in this are clean,
You dwelt in the far-off city,
With many a mile between.

You did not watch the flowing
    Of the treacherous, trickling rill;
You did not aid the growing
    Of the tiny rifts in the hill.

What if you had? I leave it,
    It is too dark a thought;
How could the heart conceive it?
    How came it, all unsought?

II.

A look of great affliction,
    As you tell what one told you,
With a feeble contradiction,
    Or a 'hope it is not true!'

A story quite too meagre
    For naming any more,
Only your friend seems eager
    To know a little more.

No doubt of explanation,
    If all was known, you see;
One might get information
    From Mrs. A. or B.

Only some simple queries
    Passed on from tongue to tongue,
Though the ever-growing series
    Has out of nothing sprung.

Only a faint suggestion,
    Only a doubtful hint,
Only a leading question
    With a special tone or tint.

Only a low 'I wonder!'
    Nothing unfair at all;
But the whisper grows to thunder,
    And a scathing bolt may fall;

And a good ship is dismasted,
    And hearts are like to break,
And a Christian life is blasted,
    For a scarcely-guessed mistake!

Leaning Over the Waterfall.

A young lady, aged 20, fell over the rocks at the Swallow Waterfall in the summer of 1873, and was lost to sight in a moment. The body was not recovered till four hours afterwards.

LEANING over the waterfall!
    Lured by the fairy sight,
Heeding not the warning call,
    Watching the foam and the flow,
Smooth and dark, or swift and bright,
Here in the shade and there in the light!
        Oh, who could know
The coming sorrow, the nearing woe!

Leaning over the waterfall!
    Only a day before
She had spoken of Jesu's wondrous call,
    As He trod the waves of Galilee.
They asked, as she gazed from the sunset shore,
'If He walked that water, what would you do?'
Then fell the answer, glad and true,
        'If He beckoned me,
I would go to Him on the pathless sea.'

Leaning over the waterfall
    Only a moment before!
And then the slip, the helpless call,
    The plunge unheard in the pauseless roar
    By the startled watchers on the shore;
And the feet that stood by the waterfall,
        So fair and free,
Are standing with Christ by the crystal sea.

Leaning over the waterfall!
    Have you not often leant
(What should hinder? or what appall?)

Freely, fearlessly, over the brink,
Merrily glancing adown the stream,
Or gazing wrapt in a musical dream
At the lovely waters? But pause and think—
Who kept *your* feet,
And suffered you not such death to meet?

Leaning over the waterfall!
What if *your* feet had slipped?
Never a moment of power to call,
Never a hand in time to save
From the terrible rush of the ruthless wave!
Hearken! would it be ill or well
If thus *you* fell?
Hearken! would it be heaven or hell?

Leaning over the waterfall!
Listen, and learn, and lean!
Listen to Him whose loving call
Soundeth deep in your heart to-day!
Learn of Jesus, the only way,
How to be holy, how to be blest!
Lean on His breast,
And yours shall be safety and joy and rest.

Forest Voices.

The forest hath its voices,
Whose sweetness aye rejoices,
Or soothes the spirit wondrously;
Borne on their leafy wings,
They tell of quiet things
And mingle in strange harmony.

There is a murmuring song,
A cadence soft and long,
Evoking dreams of still delight;
There is a clarion note,
Whose blithesome echoes float,
Chasing the darkling spells of grief and night.

There is a whispering sound
Within the forest-bound,
Telling the heart of things unseen;
That nameless holy thrill
Passeth o'er vale and hill
And through the dark and lone ravine.

It is a harp sublime
With ever-varying chime,
Awakening feelings ever new;
For, tuned by Him who made
The all-harmonious shade,
Each forest-voice is sweet and true.

The Turned Lesson.

'I THOUGHT I knew it!' she said,
'I thought I had learnt it quite!'
But the gentle Teacher shook her head,
With a grave yet loving light
In the eyes that fell on the upturned face,
As she gave the book
With the mark still set in the self-same place.

'I thought I knew it!' she said;
And a heavy tear fell down,
As she turned away with bending head,
Yet not for reproof or frown,
Not for the lesson to learn again,
Or the play-hour lost;—
It was something else that gave the pain.

She could not have put it in words,
But the Teacher understood,
As God understands the chirp of the birds
In the depth of an autumn wood.
And a quiet touch on the reddening cheek
Was quite enough;
No need to question, no need to speak.

Then the gentle voice was heard,
'Now I will try you again!'
And the lesson was mastered,—every word!
Was it not worth the pain?
Was it not kinder the task to turn,
Than to let it pass,
As a lost, lost leaf that she did not learn?

Is it not often so,
That we only learn in part,
And the Master's testing-time may show
That it was not quite 'by heart'?
Then He gives, in His wise and patient grace,
That lesson again
With the mark still set in the self-same place.

Only, stay by His side
Till the page is really known,
It may be we failed because we tried
To learn it all alone.
And now that He would not let us lose
One lesson of love
(For He knows the loss)—can we refuse?

But oh! how *could* we dream
That we knew it all so well?
Reading so fluently, as we deem,
What we could not even spell!
And oh! how could we grieve once more
That patient One
Who has turned so many a task before?

That waiting One, who now
Is letting us try again;
Watching us with the patient brow
That bore the wreath of pain;
Thoroughly teaching what He would teach,
Line upon line,
Thoroughly doing His work in each.

Then let our hearts 'be still,'
  Though our task is turned to-day.
Oh let Him teach us what He will,
  In His own gracious way,
Till, sitting only at Jesu's feet,
    As we learn each line,
The hardest is found all clear and sweet!

To Helga.

Come down, and show the dwellers far below
  What God is painting on each mountain place!
  Show His fair colours, and His perfect grace,
Dowering each blossom born of sun and snow:
His tints, not thine! Thou art God's copyist,
  O gifted Helga! His thy golden height,
  Thy purple depth, thy rosy sunset light,
Thy blue snow-shadows, and thy weird white mist.
Reveal His works to many a distant land!
  Paint for His praise, oh paint for love of Him!
He is thy Master, let Him hold thy hand,
  So thy pure heart no cloud of self shall dim.
At His dear feet lay down thy laurel-store,
Which crimson proof of thy redemption bore.

In Loyal and Loving Remembrance of H.R.H. the Princess Alice.

{Written to accompany a memorial wreath of white roses and palm leaves, painted by the Baroness Helga von Cramm.}

Two nations mourn! The same great grief is known
  By human hearts on either side the sea,
Mourning with those who yet must mourn alone
  Upon the silent height where only He
Can come and whisper comfort, who hath worn
The lonely diadem of cruel thorn.

Mourning for her whose royal love hath shown
    Secrets of comfort in the darkest days;
Who, like her Master, stooping from a throne
    The suffering or the lost could heal or raise;
Leaving, like Him, example pure and bright,
For court or cottage home a starry light.

Two nations mourn; a hand from each would lay
Fair flowers and simple verse upon her tomb to-day.

December 23rd, 1879.

Our Red-Letter Days.

My Alpine staff recalls each shining height,
    Each pass of grandeur with rejoicing gained,
    Carved with a lengthening record, self-explained,
Of mountain-memories sublime and bright.
No valley-life but hath some mountain days,
    Bright summits in the retrospective view,
    And toil-won passes to glad prospects new,
Fair sunlit memories of joy and praise.
Grave on thy heart each past 'red-letter day!'
Forget not all the sunshine of the way
By which the Lord hath led thee: answered prayers
And joys unasked; strange blessings, lifted cares,
Grand promise-echoes! Thus thy life shall be
One record of His love and faithfulness to thee.

The Awakening.

So it has come to you, dear,
    Come so soon!
Come in the sunshine early,
Come in the morning pearly,
    Not in the blaze of noon.

Yes, it has come to you, dear,
Strange and sweet;
Come ere the merry May-time
Melts to the glowing hay-time,
Hushed in the sultry heat.

Come—with mysterious shadow,
Weird and new,—
Come with a magic lustre
Hung on the shining cluster
Ripening fast for you.

Come! and the exquisite minor,
Rich and deep,
Swells with Æolian blending
Chords of the spirit, ending
Boyhood's enchanted sleep.

Sleep that is past for ever!
Is it gain?
What does the waking seem like?
Love that is only dream-like
Sings not a truthful strain.

Hearts that have roused and listened
Never more,
(Though they may miss the crossed tones,
Though they may mourn the lost tones,)
Sleep as they slept before.

Come! and the great transition
Now is past!
Never again the boy-life,
Only the pain—and joy-life,
More of the first than last.

Come! and they do not guess it,
Why such a change!
Why should the mirth and riot
Tone into manly quiet!
Is it not passing strange?

Come! 'Tis a night of wonder
At this call.
Characters cabalistic,
Writings all dim and mystic
Tremble upon the wall.

Come! am I glad or sorry?
Wait and see!
Wait for God's silent moulding,
Wait for His full unfolding,
Wait for the days to be.

Golden Land.

Far from home alone I wander
Over mountain and pathless wave,
But the fair land that shineth yonder
Claimeth the love that erst it gave.
Golden Land, so far, so nearing!
Land of those who wait for me!
Ever brighter the vision cheering,
Golden Land, I haste to thee!

On my path a golden sunlight
Softly falls where'er I roam,
And I know it is the one light
Both of exile and of home.
Golden Land, so far, so near,
On my heart engraven clear,
Though I wander from strand to strand,
Dwells my heart in that Golden Land.

April.

O the wealth of pearly blossom, O the woodland's emerald gleam!
O the welcome, welcome sunshine on the diamond-sparkling stream!
O the carol from the hawthorn and the trill from dazzling blue!
O the glory of the spring-time, making all things bright and new!

O the rosy eve's surrender
To the Easter moonlight tender!
O the early morning splendour,
    Fresh and fragrant, cool and clear,
    In the rising of the year!
O the gladness of the children after all the dismal days,
In the freedom and the beauty and the heart-rejoicing rays!
Do we chill the gleeful spirit, check the pulses bounding fast,
By the mournful doubt suggested: 'Ah, but, darling, *will it last?*'

Though we know there may be tempests, and we know there will be showers,
Yet we know they only hasten summer's richer crown of flowers.
Blossom leads to golden fruitage, bursting bud to foliage soon;
April's pleasant gleam shall strengthen to the glorious glow of June.
April leads to joyous May-time,
With its ever-lengthening day-time:
This again to joyous hay-time,
    When the harvest-home is near,
    In the zenith of the year.
So we only tell the children of the sunnier days in store,
Of the treasures and the beauties that shall open more and more.
So the silver carol rises, for the winter-time is past!
When the summer days are coming, need we ask if spring shall last?

O the gladness of the spirit, when the true and Only Light
Pours in radiant resplendence, making all things new and bright!
When the love of Jesus shineth in its overcoming power,
When the secret sweet communion hallows every passing hour.
O the calm and happy resting,
Free from every fear molesting!
O the Christ-victorious breasting
    Of the tempter's varied art,
    In the spring-time of the heart!
O the freedom and the fervour after all the faithless days!
O the ever-new thanksgiving and the ever-flowing praise!
Shall we tempt the gaze from Jesus, and a doubting shadow cast,
Satan's own dark word suggesting by the whisper '"*If*" it last'?

Though we know there must be trials and there will be tears below,
Yet we know His glorious purpose, and His promises we know!
Only ask—'What saith the Master?' and believe His word alone,
That 'from glory unto glory' He shall lead, shall change His own.

Ever more and more bestowing,
Love and joy in riper glowing,
Faith increasing, graces growing—
Such His promises to you!
He is faithful, He is true!
Each Amen becomes an anthem, for we know He will fulfil
All the purpose of His goodness, all the splendour of His will.
Only trust the living Saviour, only trust Him all the way,
And your springtide path shall brighten to the perfect summer day!

Mizpah.

MESSAGES FOR ABSENT FRIENDS.

ONLY a leaf, yet it shall bear
A wealth of love, of mintage true!
Only a simple earnest prayer,
That silently goes up for you;
Yet you and I may never know
What blessings from that prayer may flow.

'GRACE, mercy, peace.'
Triple blossom, rainbow-hued,
Fresh and fragrant, heaven-bedewed,
Brightening desert solitude,
Springing from the Love Divine,
Love that ever shall entwine
With our own, with yours and mine.

UPON the same bright morning star
Our gaze may meet, though severed far:
The Star of Bethlehem to-day
Shines brightly on our wintry way;
And, gazing on its radiance clear,
Our hearts may meet, and we are near!

As the sounding shell conveys
The murmur of the sea,
So let this tiny token raise
Some memory of me;
For loving thought of prayer and praise
Fail not to rise for thee.

THOUGH the circling flight of time may find us
Far apart, or severed more and more,
Yet the farewell always lies behind us,
And the welcome always lies before.
Meanwhile God is leading, surely, slowly,
Through the shadows with a hand of love,
To the house where, 'mid the myriads holy,
Only welcomes wait us both above.

Hymn for March 31, 1873.

BEING THE DAY APPOINTED FOR SPECIAL AND UNITED PRAYER FOR IRELAND.

'The isles shall wait upon Me, and on Mine arm shall they trust.'—ISAIAH 51:5.

FATHER, we would plead Thy promise, bending at Thy glorious throne,
That the isles shall wait upon Thee, trusting in Thine arm alone!
One bright isle we bring before Thee, while in faith Thy children pray
For a full and mighty blessing, with united voice to-day.

Gracious Saviour, look in mercy on this Island of the West,
Win the wandering and the weary with Thy pardon and Thy rest:
As the *only* Friend and Saviour let Thy blessèd name be owned,
Who hast shed Thy blood most precious, and for ever hast atoned!

Blessèd Spirit, lift Thy standard, pour Thy grace, and shed Thy light!
Lift the veil and loose the fetter; come with new and quickening might;
Make the desert places blossom, shower Thy sevenfold gifts abroad;
Make Thy servants wise and stedfast, valiant for the truth of God.

Triune God of grace and glory, be the isle for which we plead
Shielded, succoured with Thy blessing, strong in every hour of need;
Flooded with Thy truth and glory (glowing sunlight from above),
And encompassed with the ocean of Thine everlasting love.

Oh, surround Thy throne of power with Thine emerald bow of peace:
Bid the wailing, and the warring, and the wild confusion cease.
Thou remainest King for ever,—Thou shalt reign, and earth adore!
Thine the kingdom, Thine the power, Thine the glory evermore.

Reality.

'FATHER, WE KNOW THE REALITY OF JESUS CHRIST.'—
Words used by a workman in prayer.[1]

REALITY, reality,
Lord Jesus Christ, Thou art to me!
From the spectral mists and driving clouds,
From the shifting shadows and phantom crowds;
From unreal words and unreal lives,
Where truth with falsehood feebly strives;
From the passings away, the chance and change,
Flickerings, vanishings, swift and strange,
I turn to my glorious rest on Thee,
Who art the grand Reality.

Reality in greatest need,
Lord Jesus Christ, Thou art indeed!
Is the pilot real, who alone can guide
The drifting ship through the midnight tide?
Is the lifeboat real, as it nears the wreck,
And the saved ones leap from the parting deck?
Is the haven real, where the barque may flee
From the autumn gales of the wild North Sea?
Reality indeed art Thou,
My Pilot, Lifeboat, Haven now!

Reality, reality,
In brightest days art Thou to me!

[1] At another prayer meeting on the same day a young Christian who had been witnessing for this 'reality' among those who called religion a 'phantom' and a 'sham' prayed earnestly, 'Lord Jesus, let Thy dear servant write for us what Thou art—Thou living, bright Reality!' And, urging His plea with increasing vehemence, he added, 'and let her do it *this very night.*' That 'very night' these verses were flashed into my mind; while he was 'yet speaking,' they were written and *dated.* Does not this show the 'reality of prayer?'

Thou art the sunshine of my mirth,
Thou art the heaven above my earth,
The spring of the love of all my heart,
And the Fountain of my song Thou art;
For dearer than the dearest now,
And better than the best, art Thou,
    Belovèd Lord, in whom I see
    Joy-giving, glad Reality.

        Reality, reality,
    Lord Jesus, Thou hast been to me.
When I thought the dream of life was past,
And 'the Master's home-call' come at last;
When I thought I only had to wait
A little while at the Golden Gate,—
Only another day or two,
Till Thou Thyself shouldst bear me through,
    How real Thy presence was to me
    How precious Thy Reality!

        Reality, reality,
    Lord Jesus Christ, Thou art to me!
Thy name is sweeter than songs of old,
Thy words are better than 'most fine gold,'
Thy deeds are greater than hero-glory,
Thy life is grander than poet-story;
But Thou, Thyself, for aye the same,
Art more than words and life and name!
    Thyself Thou hast revealed to me,
    In glorious Reality.

        Reality, reality,
    Lord Jesus Christ, is crowned in Thee.
In Thee is every type fulfilled,
In Thee is every yearning stilled
For perfect beauty, truth, and love;
For Thou art always far above
The grandest glimpse of our Ideal,
Yet more and more we know Thee real,

And marvel more and more to see
Thine infinite Reality.

Reality, reality
Of grace and glory dwells in Thee.
How real Thy mercy and Thy might!
How real Thy love, how real Thy light!
How real Thy truth and faithfulness!
How real Thy blessing when Thou dost bless!
How real Thy coming to dwell within!
How real the triumphs Thou dost win!
Does not the loving and glowing heart
Leap up to own how real Thou art?

Reality, reality!
Such let our adoration be!
Father, we bless Thee with heart and voice,
For the wondrous grace of Thy sovereign choice.
That patiently, gently, sought us out
In the far-off land of death and doubt,
That drew us to Christ by the Spirit's might,
That opened our eyes to see the light
That arose in strange reality,
From the darkness falling on Calvary.

Reality, reality,
Lord Jesus Christ, Thou art to me!
My glorious King, my Lord, my God,
Life is too short for half the laud,
For half the debt of praise I owe
For this blest knowledge, that 'I know
The reality of Jesus Christ,'—
Unmeasured blessing, gift unpriced!
Will I not praise Thee when I see
In the long noon of Eternity,
Unveiled, Thy 'bright Reality!'

Seulement pour Toi.

[Written for and sung by some Swiss peasants at a Sunday afternoon Bible reading, July 23rd, 1876.]

Que je sois, O cher Sauveur,		*O that I be—May I be, O dear Saviour,*
Seulement à Toi!	Hosea 3:1*	*Only (wholly) to Thee (Thine)!*
Soit l'amour de tout mon cœur	Matt. 22:37	*Be the love of all my heart*
Seulement pour Toi.		*Solely for Thee.*
Je reviens à mon Père	John 14:6	*I come back to my Father*
Seulement par Toi,		*Only through Thee,*
Ma confiance entière	Psalm 118:8	*My confidence entire*
Sera en Toi,		*Wants to be (will be) in Thee,*
Seulement en Toi.		*Only in Thee.*
Le péché Tu as porté	I Peter 2:24	*The sin, Thou hast carried (borne)*
Seul, seul pour moi;		*Alone, alone for me;*
Et Ton sang Tu as versé		*And Thy blood Thou hast shed*
Seul, seul pour moi.		*Alone, alone for me.*
Toute gloire, toute joie	Rev. 5:12	*All glory, all joy,*
Sera pour Toi;		*Will be for Thee;*
L'espérance et la foi	Acts 4:12	*The hope and faith*
Seront en Toi,		*Will be in Thee,*
Seulement en Toi.		*Only in Thee.*
Aujourd'hui, O cher Seigneur,	II Cor. 6:2	*Today, O dear Lord,*
Acceptes-moi!	Ephesians. 1:6	*Accept me!*
Tu es seul mon grand Sauveur,	Isaiah 19:20	*Thou alone art my great Saviour,*
Tu es mon Roi.	Psalm 44:4	*Thou alone art my King.*
Tous mes moments, tous mes jours	II Cor.	*All my moments, all my days*
Seront pour Toi!	5:15	*Will be for Thee!*
Jésus, gardes-moi toujours	Isaiah 27:3	*Jesus, keep me always*
Seulement pour Toi,		*Only for Thee,*
Seulement pour Toi.		*Only for Thee.*
Que je chante et que je pleure	Psalm 21:13	*O that I sing and that I weep*
Seulement pour Toi!		*Only for Thee!*
Que je vive et que je meure	Romans 14:8	*Let me live and let me die*
Seulement pour Toi!		*Only for Thee!*

[1] English translation by David Chalkley.

Jésus, que m'as tant aimé	Galatians 2:20	*Jesus, how Thou hast loved me,*
Mourant pour moi,		*Dying for me,*
Toute mon éternité	I Thess. 4:17	*All my eternity*
Sera pour Toi,		*Will be for Thee,*
Seulement pour Toi.		*Only for Thee.*

A Song in the Night.

[Written in severe pain, Sunday afternoon, October 8th, 1876, at the Pension Wengen, Alps.]

I TAKE this pain, Lord Jesus,
From Thine own hand,
The strength to bear it bravely
Thou wilt command.

I am too weak for effort,
So let me rest,
In hush of sweet submission,
On Thine own breast.

I take this pain, Lord Jesus,
As proof indeed
That Thou art watching closely
My truest need:

That Thou, my Good Physician,
Art watching still;
That all Thine own good pleasure
Thou wilt fulfil.

I take this pain, Lord Jesus,
What Thou dost choose
The soul that really loves Thee
Will not refuse.

It is not for the first time
I trust to-day;
For Thee my heart has never
A trustless 'Nay!'

I take this pain, Lord Jesus,
  But what beside?
'Tis no unmingled portion
  Thou dost provide.

In every hour of faintness,
  My cup runs o'er
With faithfulness and mercy,
  And love's sweet store.

I take this pain, Lord Jesus,
  As Thine own gift,
And true though tremulous praises
  I now uplift.

I am too weak to sing them,
  But Thou dost hear
The whisper from the pillow,—
  Thou art so near!

'Tis Thy dear hand, O Saviour,
  That presseth sore,
The hand that bears the nail-prints
  For evermore.

And now beneath its shadow,
  Hidden by Thee,
The pressure only tells me
  Thou lovest me!

What Will You Do Without Him?

I COULD not do without Him!
  Jesus is more to me
Than all the richest, fairest gifts
  Of earth could ever be.
But the more I find Him precious—
  And the more I find Him true—
The more I long for you to find
  What He can be to you.

You need not do without Him,
    For He is passing by,
He is waiting to be gracious,
    Only waiting for your cry;
He is waiting to receive you—
    To make you all His own!
Why will you do without Him,
    And wander on alone?

Why will you do without Him?
    Is He not kind indeed?
Did He not die to save you?
    Is He not all you need?
Do you not want a Saviour?
    Do you not want a Friend?
One who will love you faithfully,
    And love you to the end?

Why will you do without Him?
    The word of God is true,
The world is passing to its doom—
    And you are passing too.
It may be no to-morrow
    Shall dawn on you or me;
Why will you run the awful risk
    Of all eternity?

What will you do without Him,
    In the long and dreary day
Of trouble and perplexity,
    When you do not know the way,
And no one else can help you,
    And no one guides you right,
And hope comes not with morning,
    And rest comes not with night?

You could not do without Him,
    If once He made you see
The fetters that enchain you,
    Till He hath set you free:

If once you saw the fearful load
  Of sin upon your soul—
The hidden plague that ends in death,
  Unless He makes you whole.

What will you do without Him
  When death is drawing near?
Without His love—the only love
  That casts out every fear;
When the shadow-valley opens,
  Unlighted and unknown,
And the terrors of its darkness
  Must all be passed alone!

What will you do without Him,
  When the great white throne is set,
And the Judge who never can mistake,
  And never can forget,—
The Judge whom you have never here
  As Friend and Saviour sought,
Shall summon you to give account
  Of deed and word and thought?

What will you do without Him,
  When He hath shut the door,
And you are left outside, because
  You would not come before?
When it is no use knocking,
  No use to stand and wait,
For the word of doom tolls through your heart,
  That terrible 'Too late!'

You *cannot* do without Him
  There is no other Name
By which you ever *can* be saved,
  No way, no hope, no claim!
Without Him—everlasting loss
  Of love, and life, and light!
Without Him—everlasting woe,
  And everlasting night.

But with Him—oh! *with Jesus!*
    Are any words so blest?
With Jesus, everlasting joy
    And everlasting rest!
With Jesus,—all the empty heart
    Filled with His perfect love;
With Jesus,—perfect peace below,
    And perfect bliss above.

Why should you do without Him?
    It is not yet too late;
He has not closed the day of grace,
    He has not shut the gate.
He calls you!—hush! He calls you!
    He would not have you go
Another step without Him,
    Because He loves you so.

He would not do without you!
    He calls and calls again—
'Come unto Me! Come unto Me!'
    Oh, shall He call in vain?
He wants to have you with Him;
    Do you not want Him too?
You cannot do without Him,
    And He wants—even you.

Thy Father Waits for Thee.

Wanderer from thy Father's home,
    So full of sin, so far away,
Wilt thou any longer roam?
    Oh, wilt thou not return to-day?
Wilt thou? Oh, He knows it all,
    Thy Father sees, He meets thee here!
Wilt thou? Hear His tender call,
    'Return, return!' while He is near.

He is here! His loving voice
    Hath reached thee, though so far away!
He is waiting to rejoice,
    O wandering one, o'er thee to-day.
Waiting, waiting to bestow
    His perfect pardon, full and free;
Waiting, waiting till thou know
    His wealth of love for thee, for thee!

Rise and go! Thy Father waits
    To welcome and receive and bless;
Thou shalt tread His palace gates
    In royal robe of righteousness.
Thine shall be His heart of love,
    And thine His smile, and thine His home,
Thine His joy, all joys above—
    O wandering child, no longer roam!

Will You Not Come?

WILL you not come to Him for *Life?*
    Why will ye die, oh, why?
He gave His life for you, for you!
The gift is free, the word is true!
    Will you not come? oh, why will you die?

Will you not come to Him for *Peace?*
    Peace through His cross alone!
He shed His precious blood for you;
The gift is free, the word is true!
    He is our Peace—oh, is He your own?

Will you not come to Him for *Rest?*
    All that are weary, come!
The rest He gives is deep and true,
'Tis offered now, 'tis offered you!
    Rest in His love and rest in His home.

Will you not come to Him for *Joy?*
　　Will you not come for this?
He laid His joys aside for you,
To give you joy so sweet, so true:
　　Sorrowing heart, oh, drink of the bliss!

Will you not come to Him for *Love,*
　　Love that can fill the heart?
Exceeding great, exceeding free!
He loveth you, He loveth me!
　　Will you not come? Why stand you apart?

Will you not come to Him for ALL?
　　Will you not 'taste and see'?
He waits to give it all to you,
The gifts are free, the words are true!
　　Jesus is calling, 'Come unto Me!'

'The Shining Light, That Shineth More and More unto the Perfect Day.'

PROVERBS 4:18.

A YEAR ago the gold light
　　Sweet morning made for me;
A tender and untold light,
　　Like music on the sea.
Light and music twining
　　In melodious glory,
A rare and radiant shining
　　On my changing story.

To-day the golden sunlight
　　Is full and broad and strong;
The glory of the One light
　　Must overflow in song;
Song that floweth ever,
　　Sweeter every day,
Song whose echoes never,
　　Never die away.

How shall the light be clearer
That is so bright to-day?
How shall the hope be dearer
That pours such joyous ray?
I am only waiting
For the answer golden,
What faith is antedating
Shall not be withholden.

Church Missionary Jubilee Hymn.

'He shall see of the travail of His soul, and shall be satisfied.'—Isaiah 53:11.

Rejoice with Jesus Christ to-day,
All ye who love His holy sway!
The travail of His soul is past,
He shall be satisfied at last.

Rejoice with Him, rejoice indeed,
For He shall see His chosen seed!
But ours the trust, the grand employ,
To work out this divinest joy.

Of all His own He loseth none,
They shall be gathered one by one;
He gathereth the smallest grain,
His travail shall not be in vain.

Arise and work! arise and pray
That He would haste the dawning day!
And let the silver trumpet sound,
Wherever Satan's slaves are found.

The vanquished foe shall soon be stilled,
The conquering Saviour's joy fulfilled,
Fulfilled in us, fulfilled in them,
His crown, His royal diadem.

Soon, soon our waiting eyes shall see
The Saviour's mighty Jubilee!
His harvest-joy is filling fast,
He shall be satisfied at last!

A Happy New Year to You.

New mercies, new blessings, new light on thy way;
New courage, new hope, and new strength for each day;
New notes of thanksgiving, new chords of delight,
New praise in the morning, new songs in the night;
New wine in thy chalice, new altars to raise;
New fruits for thy Master, new garments of praise;
New gifts from His treasures, new smiles from His face;
New streams from the fountain of infinite grace;
New stars for thy crown, and new tokens of love;
New gleams of the glory that waits thee above;
New light of His countenance full and unpriced;—
All this be the joy of thy new life in Christ!

Another Year.

Another year is dawning!
Dear Master, let it be,
In working or in waiting,
Another year with Thee.

Another year of leaning
Upon Thy loving breast,
Of ever-deepening trustfulness,
Of quiet, happy rest.

Another year of mercies,
Of faithfulness and grace;
Another year of gladness
In the shining of Thy face.

Another year of progress,
  Another year of praise;
Another year of proving
  Thy presence 'all the days.'

Another year of service,
  Of witness for Thy love;
Another year of training
  For holier work above.

Another year is dawning,
  Dear Master, let it be,
On earth, or else in heaven,
  Another year for Thee!

New Year's Wishes.

WHAT shall I wish thee?
  Treasures of earth?
Songs in the spring-time,
  Pleasure and mirth?
Flowers on thy pathway,
  Skies ever clear?
Would this ensure thee
  A Happy New Year?

What shall I wish thee?
  What can be found
Bringing thee sunshine
  All the year round?
Where is the treasure,
  Lasting and dear,
That shall ensure thee
  A Happy New Year?

Faith that increaseth,
  Walking in light;
Hope that aboundeth,
  Happy and bright;

Love that is perfect,
    Casting out fear;—
These shall ensure thee
    A Happy New Year.

Peace in the Saviour,
    Rest at His feet,
Smile of His countenance
    Radiant and sweet,
Joy in His presence,
    Christ ever near!—
This will ensure thee
    A Happy New Year!

'Forgiven—Even Until Now.'

(Numbers 14:19.)

For New Year's Day 1879.

'Thou hast forgiven—even until now!'
    We bless Thee, Lord, for this,
And take Thy great forgiveness as we bow
    In depth of sorrowing bliss;
While over all the long, regretful past
This veil of wondrous grace Thy sovereign hand doth cast.

'Forgiven until now!' For Jesus died
    To take our sins away;
His Blood was shed, and still the infinite tide
    Flows full and deep to-day.
He paid the debt; we own it, and go free!
The cancelled bond is cast in Love's unfathomed sea.

'Forgiven until now!' For God is true,
    Faithful and just is He!
Forgiving, cleansing, making all things new!
    'Who is a God like Thee?'
O precious blood of Christ, that saves and heals,
While all its cleansing might the Holy Ghost reveals.

Yes, 'even until now!' And so we stand,
Forgiven, loved, and blessed;
And, covered in the shadow of God's hand,
Believing, are at rest.
The one great load is lifted from the soul,
That henceforth on the Lord all burdens we may roll.

Yes, 'even until now!' Then let us press
With free and willing feet
Along the King's highway of holiness,
Until we gain the street
Of golden crystal, praising purely when
We see our pardoning Lord; forgiven until then!

Matthew 14:23.

It is the quiet evening time, the sun is in the west,
And earth enrobed in purple glow awaits her nightly rest;
The shadows of the mountain peaks are lengthening o'er the sea,
And the flowerets close their eyelids on the shore of Galilee.
The multitude are gone away, their restless hum doth cease,
The birds have hushed their music, and all is calm and peace;
But on the lowly mountain side is One, whose beauteous brow
The impress bears of sorrow and of weariness e'en now.
The livelong day in deeds of love and power He hath spent,
And with them words of grace and life hath ever sweetly blent.
Now He hath gained the mountain top, He standeth all alone,
No mortal may be near Him in that hour of prayer unknown.
He prayeth.—But for whom? For Himself He needeth nought;
Nor strength, nor peace, nor pardon, where of sin there is no spot;
But 'tis for us in powerful prayer He spendeth all the night,
That His own loved ones may be kept and strengthened in the fight;
That they may all be sanctified, and perfect made in one;
That they His glory may behold where they shall need no sun;
That in eternal gladness they may be His glorious bride:
It is for this that He hath climbed the lonely mountain side.
It is for this that He denies His weary head the rest
Which e'en the foxes in their holes, and birds have in their nest.
The echo of that prayer hath died upon the rocky hill,
But on a higher, holier mount that Voice is pleading still;

For while one weary child of His yet wanders here below,
While yet one thirsting soul desires His peace and love to know,
And while one fainting spirit seeks His holiness to share,
The Saviour's loving heart shall pour a tide of mighty prayer;
Yes! till each ransomed one hath gained His home of joy and peace,
That Fount of Blessings all untold shall never, never cease.

Matthew 26:30.

'And when they had sung an hymn, they went out.'

THE sun hath gilded Judah's hills
With his last gorgeous beam;
Ghost-like the still grey mists arise
From Jordan's sacred stream.
The stars, bright flowers of the sky,
Unfold their beauties now,
And gaze on Salem's marble fane,[1]
By Olivet's dark brow.
In David's city sound is hushed
And tread of busy feet,
For solemnly his sons have met
The paschal lamb to eat.
But list! the silence of the hour
Is broken; the still air
A melody hath caught which far
Its viewless pinions bear.
Unwonted sweetness hath the strain,
And as its numbers flow,
More tender and more touching yet
Its harmony doth grow.
Not royal David's tuneful harp
Such thrilling power had known
To wake deep echoes in the soul,
As its scarce earthly tone.
Within an 'upper room' are met
A small, yet faithful band,
On whom a deep yet chastened grief
Hath laid its softening hand.

[1] fane: temple

Among them there is One who wears
  A more than mortal mien,
'Tis He on whom in all distress
  The weary one may lean.
Mysterious sadness, on that brow
  So pure and calm, doth lie;
And untold stores of deepest love
  Are beaming from His eye.
What wonder if the strain was sweet
  Above all other lays?
Seraphic well might seem the hymn
  Which Jesu's voice did raise.
The angels hush their lyres, and bend
  To hear the thrilling tone,
And heaven is silent,—with that song
  They mingle not their own.
The sorrowing ones around have heard
  Their blessèd Master tell,
That He with them no longer now
  As heretofore may dwell.
And they have sadly shared with Him
  The last, last evening meal,
And heard the last sweet comfort which
  Their mourning hearts may heal.
They do not know the fearful storm
  Which on His head must burst;
They know not all—He hath not told
  His loving ones the worst.
How could He? E'en an angel's mind
  Could never comprehend
The weight of woe, 'neath which for us
  The Saviour's head must bend;
Ere long the voice, which waketh now
  Such touching melody,
Shall cry, 'My God, My God, oh why
  Hast Thou forsaken Me?'
The hour is come; but ere they meet
  Its terrors,—yet once more
Their voices blend with His who sang
  As none e'er sang before.

Why do they linger on that note?
　Why thus the sound prolong?
Ah! 'twas the last! 'Tis ended now,
　That strangely solemn song.
And forth they go:—the song is past;
　But, like the rose-leaf, still,
Whose fragrance doth not die away,
　Its soft low echoes thrill
Through many a soul, and there awake
　New strains of glowing praise
To Him who, on that fateful eve,
　That last sweet hymn did raise.

To John Henry C — on His Third Birthday.

Blessings on thee, darling boy,
Peace and love and gentle joy!
May the coronal they twine
Through the dream of life be thine!

Little hast thou known of life,
Of its sorrow, of its strife,
Thine not yet dark Future's blast,
Thine not yet a shadowy Past.

While we reck of coming years,
Strangely mingling hopes and fears,
What are sober thoughts to thee,
In the tide of birthday glee!

Thou art beautiful and bright,
Daily wakening new delight,
Would that we the prize could hold,
Always keep thee three years old!

No, not always; thou may'st be
Something brighter yet to see,
Noble-hearted, lofty-souled,
When more years have o'er thee rolled.

Love is watching round thee now,
Tracing sunbeams on thy brow;
Never be her mission done
To thy father's only son!

Yet a higher, deeper love
Watcheth o'er thee from above
Then thy fount of motive be
Love to Him who loveth thee.

Darling, may thy years below
Like a strain of music flow,
Ever sweeter, purer, higher,
Till it swell the angel choir.

Be thy life a star of light,
Glistening through earth's stormy night,
Shining then with glorious ray
Through the One Eternal Day!

'Coming of Age.'

(J. H. S.)

What do we seek for him to-day, who, through such golden gates
Of mirth and gladness, enters now where life before him waits?
'Mid light and flowers the feast is spread, and young and old rejoice,
And motto texts speak out for all, with earnest, loving voice.

The threefold blessing Israel heard three thousand years ago,
Oh! grant it may on him to-day in power and fulness flow;
For, faithful and unchangeable, each word of God is sure,
Though heaven and earth shall pass away, His promises endure.

The Angel of the Covenant, redeeming from all ill
Both son and father, bless the lad, and every prayer fulfil;
Nor only bless, but make him, too, a blessing, Lord, from Thee:
With length of days, oh, satisfy; let him Thy glory see.

Through all the journey of his life, Thy presence with him go;
Rest *in* Thee here, and *with* Thee there, do Thou, O Lord, bestow.
Oh, keep him faithful unto death, then grant to him, we pray,
The crown of glory and of life, that fadeth not away.

So shall the father's soul be glad for him he holds so dear,
A son whose heart is truly wise in God's most holy fear;
And hallowed be our festal joy with gratitude and praise;
Forget not all His benefits, whose kindness crowns our days.

Then glory in the highest be to Him, our Strength and Song;
May every heart uplift its part, in blessings deep and long.
Through Him who died that we might live, our thanks to God ascend,
The King of kings, and Lord of lords, our Saviour and our Friend.

Evelyn.

DYING? Evelyn, darling!
        Dying? can it be?
Spring so joyous all around,
Such a spring, so early crowned,
Heralding all summer glee,
Life for everything but thee!
        Evelyn, darling, dying?
Yet it is no phantom sound,
Though the word is haunting me;
        Thou art lying
Now where life and death do meet,
Thorny path and golden street.
I thought I had no heart to write,
    But the pencil near me lay,
    Which has traced me many a day,
Dipped in colours dark or bright,
Lays I guessed would meet the sight
    Of at least some loving eye,
And perchance be heard again,
    Winning echoes far and nigh,
    Touching chords of sympathy

In the weary souls of men.
And I took it in my hand,
    For it seemed to be relief,
    After this long week of grief,
Just to let the thought expand,
And the word that haunted me
Just to write; though none shall see
What is written, only He
Who is gently leading thee,
    Evelyn, darling, without fears,
Through the vale of death,—and me
    Through the vale of tears.

All so calm;—a hazy veil
    Falling on the golden west;
Silence, like a minstrel pale,
    Preluding the Sabbath rest.
There is night before the dawn
Rise for *us* of Sabbath morn:
Is there any night for *thee*
Ere thine eyes the glory see?
Are the angels, bright and strong,
    Bearing thy free soul away,
Teaching thee the glad new song,
    On the grand star-paven way?
Art thou even now at rest,
Lying on the Saviour's breast?
Evelyn, darling, is it so?
Would, oh, would that I could know!
I can only wait in sorrow
For the tidings of the morrow.

Evelyn, darling, laid so low!
Only three short months ago
Thou wert full of life and glee,
Round the laden Christmas tree;
Foremost in the carol-singing,
Fun and frolic gaily flinging.
Tallest, fairest of the troop,
Opening rose on slender stem,

Reigning 'mid the bright-eyed group,
    Queen without a diadem;
In thy robe of snowy sheen,
Decked with silken emerald green.
Few there are who ever knew
    Merrier holidays than thine,
Whether summer breezes blew,
    Or the winter stars did shine.
Evelyn, darling, can it be,
    Was that Christmas tree the last?
How believe it, that for thee
    Christmas holidays are past!
And that summer leaves will wave,
    And the Easter moon will shine,
Over the first household grave,
        First,—and *thine!*

I am not praying,—prayer is hushed,
    God's hand is laid upon my heart;
The earthly hope for ever crushed,
    The heavenly *answered,* not in part,
But fully, perfectly! I prayed
    For life, and He hath given the life
Which triumphs o'er the grave's cold shade;
    For peace, and He hath ended strife
And spoken love. There have been tears
And earnest pleadings through long years;
But He is faithful to His word,
I *know* at last that He has heard.
But not, oh not as I had thought
    In ignorant and selfish love,
The Master calls,—she tarries not,
    For He hath need of her above.
The lambs He gathers with His arm
No grief, no sin, no death can harm,
So safely folded on His breast,
For ever and for ever blest.
Could God Himself give more? His will
Is best, though we are weeping still.

Yet the old cry comes again,
Evelyn, darling, dying!
Is it true, or is it dreaming?
Is it only ghastly seeming
Of a sorrow far away,
Not to fall for many a day?
If I saw thee lying,
I might realize it so!
Last I saw thee in the glow
Of thy brightest health and bloom;
Was it only for the tomb?
Then the sorrow grows with this—
Not a word of fond good-bye,
Not one tender parting kiss,
Not one glance of loving eye!
Well I know it could not be!
God's appointed way for me
Was assuredly—'Be still,
Wait in silence for His will.'
Father, I have said Amen,
Said it often, now again!
Father, strengthen it and seal!
Let my weary spirit feel
I am very near to Thee,
For Thy hand is laid on me,—
Though the shadows gather deep,
Thou canst calm and aid and keep.

Father, where the shadows fall
Deeper yet, deepest of all,
Send Thy peace, and show Thy power
In affliction's direst hour;
To each mourning heart draw near,
Soothe and bless, sustain and cheer.
Thou *wilt* hear, I know not *how!*
Thou canst help, 'and only Thou.'
This my prayer I leave with Thee.
Father! hear and answer me
For the sake of Him who knows
All our love and all our woes.

Faithful Promises.

NEW YEAR'S HYMN.

ISAIAH 41:10.

STANDING at the portal
Of the opening year,
Words of comfort meet us,
Hushing every fear.
Spoken through the silence
By our Father's voice,
Tender, strong, and faithful,
Making us rejoice.
Onward, then, and fear not,
Children of the Day!
For His word shall never,
Never pass away!

I, the Lord, am with thee,
Be thou not afraid!
I will help and strengthen,
Be thou not dismayed!
Yea, I will uphold thee
With My own Right Hand;
Thou art called and chosen
In my sight to stand.
Onward, then, and fear not,
Children of the Day!
For His word shall never,
Never pass away!

For the year before us,
Oh, what rich supplies!
For the poor and needy
Living streams shall rise;
For the sad and sinful
Shall His grace abound;
For the faint and feeble
Perfect strength be found.
Onward, then, and fear not,
Children of the Day!

For His word shall never,
Never pass away!

He will never fail us,
He will not forsake;
His eternal covenant
He will never break!
Resting on His promise,
What have we to fear?
God is all-sufficient
For the coming year.
Onward, then, and fear not.
Children of the Day!
For His word shall never,
Never pass away!

The Maidens of England.

On the presentation of a Bible to their Princess Royal.

Ere the pathless ocean waters
Bear thee far from England's shore,
Come we, England's youthful daughters,
Warmly greeting thee once more.

Rarest jewels, lustre flinging,
Grace thy royal diadem;
Yet we come, an offering bringing
Richer than its richest gem.

While with prayerful love unspoken,
Princess! glows each maiden heart,
Deign to take this sacred token,
Brightest lamp and surest chart.

May its holy precepts guide thee
In each hour of joy or sadness;
Yet may he who stands beside thee
Share with thee unfading gladness.

Ever on thy pathway shining,
Living stars 'mid earthly night,
May its peace and grace entwining
Gird thee with a robe of light.

Rose of England! fragrance breathing,
To thy far new home depart,
Round thy early bloom enwreathing
All the love of England's heart.

Be thy gladness ever vernal
'Mid the wintry scenes below,
Till a crown of life eternal
Gleams upon thy royal brow!

Father, be Thou ever near her!
Saviour, fill her with Thy love!
Let Thy constant presence cheer her,
Joy-imparting Holy Dove!

Scotland's Welcome to H.R.H. Princess Louise.

Sweet Rose of the South! contented to rest
In the fair island home which thy presence has blessed:
From the Highlands resounding, glad welcome shall float,
And the Lowlands re-echo the jubilant note.

Merry England has loved thee and cherished thee long,
Her blessings go with thee in prayer and in song;
Bonnie Scotland has won thee, and lays at thy feet
Love tender and fervent, love loyal and sweet.

Chorus.—Our own bonnie Scotland with welcome shall ring,
While greeting and homage we loyally bring;
The crown of our love shall thy diadem be,
And the throne of our hearts is waiting for thee.

Then come, like the sunrise that gilds with a smile
The dark mountains and valleys of lonely Argyle;
Golden splendour shall fall on the pale northern snow,
And with roselight of love the purple shall glow.

Though the voice that should bless, and the hand that should seal,
Is 'away,' and at rest in 'the land o' the leal,'
May the God of thy father look graciously down,
With blessings on blessings thy gladness to crown.

Chorus.—Our own bonnie Scotland with welcome shall ring,
While greeting and homage we loyally bring;
The crown of our love shall thy diadem be,
And the throne of our hearts is waiting for thee.

Chosen Lessons.

'Him shall He teach in the way that He shall choose.'—Psalm 25:12.

In the way that He shall choose
He will teach us;
Not a lesson we shall lose,
All shall reach us.

Strange and difficult indeed
We may find it,
But the blessing that we need
Is behind it.

All the lessons He shall send
Are the sweetest,
And His training, in the end,
Is completest.

Hitherto and Henceforth.

"The Lord has blessed me hitherto." —Joshua 17:14

Hitherto the Lord hath helped us,
Guiding all the way;
Henceforth let us trust Him fully,
Trust Him all the day.

Hitherto the Lord hath loved us,
  Caring for His own;
Henceforth let us love Him better,
  Live for Him alone.

Hitherto the Lord hath blessed us,
  Crowning all our days;
Henceforth let us live to bless Him,
  Live to show His praise.

Christmas Gifts.

'Thou hast received gifts for men.'—Psalm 68:18.

  Christmas gifts for thee,
    Fair and free!
Precious things from the heavenly store,
Filling thy casket more and more;
Golden love in divinest chain,
That never can be untwined again;
Silvery carols of joy that swell
Sweetest of all in the heart's lone cell;
Pearls of peace that were sought for thee
In the terrible depths of a fiery sea;
Diamond promises sparkling bright,
Flashing in farthest reaching light.

  Christmas gifts for thee,
    Grand and free!
Christmas gifts from the King of love,
Brought from His royal home above;
Brought to thee in the far-off land,
Brought to thee by His own dear hand.
Promises held by Christ for thee,
Peace as a river flowing free,
Joy that in His own joy must live,
And love that Infinite Love can give.
Surely thy heart of hearts uplifts
Carols of praise for such Christmas gifts!

He Hath Done It!

'I have blotted out, as a thick cloud, thy transgressions, and, as a cloud, thy sins: return unto Me; for I have redeemed thee. Sing, O ye heavens; for the Lord hath done it.'—Isaiah 44:22, 23.

'I know that, whatsoever God doeth, it shall be for ever: nothing can be put to it, nor anything taken from it.'—Ecclesiastes 3:14.

Sing, O heavens! the Lord hath done it!
Sound it forth o'er land and sea!
Jesus says, 'I have redeemed thee,
Now return, return to Me.'
Oh return, for His own life-blood
Paid the ransom, made us free
Evermore and evermore.

For I know that what He doeth
Stands for ever, fixed and true;
Nothing can be added to it,
Nothing left for us to do;
Nothing can be taken from it,
Done for me and done for you,
Evermore and evermore.

Listen now! the Lord hath done it!
For He loved us unto death;
It is finished! He has saved us!
Only trust to what He saith.
He hath done it! Come and bless Him,
Spend in praise your ransomed breath
Evermore and evermore.

O believe the Lord hath done it!
Wherefore linger? wherefore doubt?
All the cloud of black transgression
He Himself hath blotted out.
He hath done it! Come and bless Him,
Swell the grand thanksgiving shout
Evermore and evermore.

What Thou Wilt.

Do what Thou wilt! Yes, only do
What seemeth good to Thee:
Thou art so loving, wise, and true,
It must be best for me.

Send what Thou wilt; or beating shower,
Soft dew, or brilliant sun;
Alike in still or stormy hour,
My Lord, Thy will be done.

Teach what Thou wilt; and make me learn
Each lesson full and sweet,
And deeper things of God discern
While sitting at Thy feet.

Say what Thou wilt; and let each word
My quick obedience win;
Let loyalty and love be stirred
To deeper glow within.

Give what Thou wilt; for then I know
I shall be rich indeed;
My King rejoices to bestow
Supply for every need.

Take what Thou wilt, belovèd Lord,
For I have all in Thee!
My own exceeding great reward,
Thou, Thou Thyself shalt be!

The Key Found.

THERE is a strange wild wail around, a wail of wild unrest,
A moaning in the music, with echoes unconfessed,
And a mocking twitter here and there, with small notes shrill and thin,
And deep, low, shuddering groans that rise from caves of gloom within.

And still the weird wail crosses the harmonies of God,
And still the wailers wander through His fair lands, rich and broad;
Grave thought-explorers swell the cry of doubt and nameless pain,
And careless feet, among the flowers, trip to the dismal strain.

They may wander as they will in the hopeless search for truth,
They may squander in the quest all the freshness of their youth,
They may wrestle with the nightmares of sin's unresting sleep,
They may cast a futile plummet in the heart's unfathomed deep:

But they wait and wail and wander in vain and still in vain,
Though they glory in the dimness and are proud of very pain;
For a life of Titan struggle is but one sublime mistake,
While the spell-dream is upon them, and they cannot, will not wake.

Awake, O thou that sleepest! The Deliverer is near!
Arise, go forth to meet Him! Bow down, for He is here!
Ye shall count your true existence from this first, blessèd tryst,
For He waiteth to reveal Himself, the Very God in Christ.

For the soul is never satisfied, the life is incomplete,
And the symphonies of sorrow find no cadence calm and sweet,
And the earth-lights never lead us beyond the shadows grim,
And the lone heart never resteth till it findeth rest in Him.

Do ye doubt our feeble witness? Though ye scorn us, come and see!
Come and hear Him for yourselves, and ye shall know that it is He!
Ye shall find in Him the Centre, the Very Truth and Life,
Resplendent resolution of the endless doubt and strife.

Ye shall find a perfect fitness with your highest, deepest thought,
In Him, the fair Ideal, that so long ye vainly sought,
In Him the grand Reality ye never found before,
In Him the Lord that ye must love, the God ye must adore.

Ye shall find in Him the filling of the 'aching void' within;
In Him the instant antidote for anguish and for sin;
In Him the conscious meeting of the soul's unuttered need;
In Him the *All* that ye have sought, the goal of life indeed.

As the light is to the eye, with its sensitive array
Of delicate adjustments with their finely balanced play,
With its instinct of perception, and its craving for the light,
So is Jesus to the spirit, when He gives the inward sight.

As the full and clear translation of some characters of fate,
With their sibylline enfoldings, of dim mysterious weight,
And a haunting terror lest the real be darker than the guessed!
So is Jesus to the questions and enigmas of the breast.

As the key is to the lock, when it enters quick and true,
Fitting all the complex wards that are hidden from the view,
Moving all the secret springs that no other finds or moves,
So is Jesus to the soul, when His saving power He proves.

As the music to the ear, when the mightiest anthems roll,
With its corridors conveying every echo to the soul,
With its exquisite discernment of vibration and of tone,—
So is Jesus to the heart that is made for Him alone.

No need to prove the sunshine when the eye receives the light!
When the cipher is deciphered, we know the clue is right;
The key is known by fitting the strange intricate wards;
And the ears must own the music when they recognise the chords.

No need to prove a Saviour, when once the heart believes,
And the light of God's own glory in Jesus Christ receives!
No need for weary puzzle, with heart-lore strange and dim,
When we find our dark enigmas are simply solved in Him!

We cannot doubt our finding the very Key indeed,
When Jesus fills up every void, responds to every need,
When all the secrets of our hearts before Him are revealed,
And all the mystery of life, alone with Him, unsealed.

We cannot doubt, when once the ear of listening faith has heard,
With all-responsive thrill of love, the music of His word!
He gives the witness that excels all argument or sign,—
When we have heard it for ourselves we *know* it is Divine!

And then, oh, then the wail is stilled, the wandering is o'er,
The rest is gained, the certainty that never wavers more;
And then the full, unquivering praise arises glad and strong,
And life becomes the prelude of the everlasting song!

(HER LAST BIRTHDAY.)

The Song of a Summer Stream.

A FEW months ago
I was singing through the snow,
Though the dead brown boughs gave no hope of summer shoots,
And my persevering fall
Seemed to be no use at all,
For the hard, hard frost would not let me reach the roots.

Then the mists hung chill
All along the wooded hill,
And the cold, sad fog through my lonely dingles crept;
I was glad I had no power
To awake one tender flower
To a sure, swift doom! I would rather that it slept.

Still I sang all alone
In the sweet old summer tone,
For the strong white ice could not hush me for a day;
Though no other voice was heard
But the bitter breeze that whirred
Past the gaunt, grey trunks on its wild and angry way.

So the dim days sped,
While everything seemed dead,
And my own poor flow seemed the only living sign;
And the keen stars shone
When the freezing night came on,
From the far, far heights, all so cold and crystalline.

A few months ago
I was singing through the snow!
But now the blessed sunshine is filling all the land,
And the memories are lost
Of the winter fog and frost,
In the presence of the Summer with her full and glowing hand.

Now the woodlark comes to drink
At my cool and pearly brink,
And the ladyfern is bending to kiss my rainbow foam;
And the wild-rose buds entwine
With the dark-leaved bramble-vine,
And the centuried oak is green around the bright-eyed squirrel's home.

O the full and glad content,
That my little song is blent
With the all-melodious mingling of the choristers around!
I no longer sing alone
Through a chill surrounding moan,
For the very air is trembling with its wealth of summer sound.

Though the hope seemed long deferred,
Ere the south wind's whisper heard
Gave a promise of the passing of the weary winter days,
Yet the blessing was secure,
For the summer time was sure
When the lonely songs are gathered in the mighty choir of praise.

Hope.

What though the blossom fall and die?
The flower is not the root;
The sun of love may ripen yet
The Master's pleasant fruit.

What though by many a sinful fall
Thy garments are defiled?
A Saviour's blood can cleanse them all;
Fear not! thou art His child.

Arise! and, leaning on His strength,
Thy weakness shall be strong;
And He will teach Thy heart at length
A new perpetual song.

Arise! to follow in His track
Each holy footprint clear,

And on an upward course look back
With every brightening year.

Arise! and on thy future way
His blessing with thee be!
His presence be thy staff and stay,
Till Thou His glory see.

Fear Not.

Isaiah 43:1–7.

Listen! for the Lord hath spoken!
'Fear thou not,' saith He;
'When thou passest through the waters,
I will be with thee.

'Fear not! for I have redeemed thee;
All My sheep I know!
When thou passest through the rivers,
They shall not o'erflow.

'Fear not! by thy name I called thee,—
Mine thy heart hath learned;
When thou walkest through the fire,
Thou shalt not be burned.

'Thou art Mine! oh, therefore fear not!
Mine for ever now!
And the flame shall never kindle
On thy sealèd brow.

'Thou art precious, therefore fear not,
Precious unto Me!
I have made thee for My glory,
I have lovèd thee.'

The Scripture Cannot Be Broken.

John 10:35.

Upon the Word I rest,
Each pilgrim day;
This golden staff is best
For all the way.
What Jesus Christ hath spoken,
Can*not* be broken!

Upon the Word I rest,
So strong, so sure,
So full of comfort blest,
So sweet, so pure!
The charter of salvation,
Faith's broad foundation.

Upon the Word I stand!
That cannot die!
Christ seals it in my hand,
He cannot lie!
The word that faileth never!
Abiding ever!

Chorus. The Master hath said it! Rejoicing in this,
We ask not for sign or for token;
His word is enough for our confident bliss,—
'The Scripture *cannot* be broken!'

Nothing to Pay.

Nothing to pay! Ah, nothing to pay!
Never a word of excuse to say!
Year after year thou hast filled the score,
Owing thy Lord still more and more.
Hear the voice of Jesus say,
'Verily thou hast nothing to pay!
Ruined, lost art thou, and yet
I forgave thee all that debt.'

Nothing to pay! the debt is so great;
What will you do with the awful weight?
How shall the way of escape be made?
Nothing to pay! yet it must be paid!
    Hear the voice of Jesus say,
'Verily thou hast nothing to pay!
All has been put to My account,
I have paid the full amount.'

Nothing to pay; yes, nothing to pay!
Jesus has cleared all the debt away;
Blotted it out with His bleeding hand!
Free and forgiven and loved you stand.
    Hear the voice of Jesus say,
'Verily thou hast nothing to pay!

'He Suffered.'

'HE suffered!' Was it, Lord, indeed for me,
    The Just One for the unjust, Thou didst bear
    The weight of sorrow that I hardly dare
To look upon, in dark Gethsemane?
'He suffered!' Thou, my near and gracious Friend,
    And yet my Lord, my God! Thou didst not shrink
    For me that full and fearful cup to drink,
Because Thou lovedst even to the end!
'He suffered!' Saviour, was Thy love so vast
    That mysteries of unknown agony,
    Even unto death, its only gauge could be,
Unmeasured as the fiery depths it passed?
Lord, by the sorrows of Gethsemane,
Seal Thou my quivering love for ever unto Thee!

Behold Your King.

'Behold, and see if there be any sorrow like unto My sorrow.'—LAMENTATIONS 1:12.

BEHOLD your King! Though the moonlight steals
Through the silvery sprays of the olive tree,
No star-gemmed sceptre or crown it reveals,
In the solemn shade of Gethsemane.
Only a form of prostrate grief,
Fallen, crushed, like a broken leaf!
Oh, think of His sorrow! that we may know
The depth of love in the depth of woe.

Behold your King! Is it nothing to you,
That the crimson tokens of agony
From the kingly brow must fall like dew,
Through the shuddering shades of Gethsemane?
Jesus Himself, the Prince of Life,
Bows in mysterious mortal strife;
Oh, think of His sorrow! that we may know
The unknown love in the unknown woe.

Behold your King, with His sorrow crowned,
Alone, alone in the valley is He!
The shadows of death are gathering round,
And the Cross must follow Gethsemane.
Darker and darker the gloom must fall,
Filled is the Cup, He must drink it all!
Oh, think of His sorrow! that we may know
His wondrous love in His wondrous woe.

NOTE.—After F.R.H.'s MS. copy of 'Adoration,' written Dec. 31, 1866, she adds:—'I find this is exactly my hundredth poem, beginning from my No. 2 MS. book, and not reckoning juvenile pieces before I left school. I am not sorry that "Adoration" happens to close the round number as well as the year 1866. I should like the same subject, only better treated, to *close* my verse-writing for *life*. One would wish one's last poem to be some expression of praise to the Crucified One.'

It is a remarkable coincidence that 'Behold your King,' and 'He Suffered,' are the *closing* poems in F.R.H.'s book, written in pencil, 1879.

An Easter Prayer.

Oh let me know
The power of Thy resurrection;
Oh let me show
Thy risen life in calm and clear reflection;
Oh let me soar
Where Thou, my Saviour Christ, art gone before;
In mind and heart
Let me dwell always, only, where Thou art.

Oh let me give
Out of the gifts Thou freely givest;
Oh let me live
With life abundantly because Thou livest;
Oh make me shine
In darkest places, for Thy light is mine;
Oh let me be
A faithful witness for Thy truth and Thee.

Oh let me show
The strong reality of gospel story;
Oh let me go
From strength to strength, from glory unto glory,
Oh let me sing
For very joy, because Thou art my King;
Oh let me praise
Thy love and faithfulness through all my days.

Easter Dawn.

It is too calm to be a dream,
Too gravely sweet, too full of power,
Prayer changed to praise this very hour!
Yes, heard and answered! though it seem
Beyond the hope of yesterday,
Beyond the faith that dared to pray,

Yet not beyond the love that heard,
And not beyond the faithful word
On which each trembling prayer may rest,
And win the answer truly best.

Yes, heard and answered! sought and found!
I breathe a golden atmosphere
Of solemn joy, and seem to hear
Within, above, and all around,
The chime of deep cathedral bells,
An early herald peal that tells
A glorious Easter tide begun;
While yet are sparkling in the sun
Large raindrops of the night storm passed,
And days of Lent are gone at last.

Written in pencil the early dawn of her last Easter Day, April 1879.

The Seed of Song.

THE seed of a song was cast
On the listening hearts around,
And the sweetly winning sound
In a few short minutes passed.
But a song of perfect praise,
And a song of perfect love
Was the harvest after many days,
Beneath the everlasting rays
Of the summer-time above.

The seed of a single word
Fell among the furrows deep,
In their silent, wintry sleep,
And the sower never an echo heard.
But the 'Come!' was not in vain,
For that germ of Life and Love,
And the blessèd Spirit's quickening rain,
Made a golden sheaf of precious grain
For the Harvest Home above.

Will you not sow that song?
    Will you not drop that word
    Till the coldest hearts be stirred
From their slumber deep and long?
Then your harvest shall abound
    With rejoicing full and grand,
Where the heavenly summer-songs resound,
And the fruits of faithful work are found,
    In the Glorious Holy Land.

"Behold, the Bridegroom cometh!"

MATTHEW 25:6.

O herald whisper falling
    Upon the passing night,
Mysteriously calling
    The Children of the Light!

He cometh; oh He cometh!
    Our own belovèd Lord!
This blessed hope up-summeth
    Our undeserved reward.

He cometh! Though the hour
    Nor earth nor heaven may know,
Sure is the word of power,
    "He cometh!" Even so!

1879.

Unfinished Fragments.

THE Master will guide the weary feet,
    Choosing for each, and choosing aright
The noontide rest in the summer heat:
    For some the glory of Alpine height,
For some the breezes fresh and free
And the changeful charm of wave and sea;
For some the hush and the soothing spells
Of harvest fields and woodland dells;

For some it may be the quiet gloom
Of the suffering couch in shaded room.
Master, *our* Master, oh let it be
That our leisure and rest be still with Thee,
With Thee and *for* Thee each sunny hour.

. . . .

In pencil, May 1879.

'Arise, depart! for this is not your rest!'
The Voice fell strangely on the sleeping fold,
As fell the starlight's quivering gold
Upon the dusky lake's untroubled breast,
And yet the Shepherd's hand had led them there,
And made them to lie down amid the pastures fair.

'Arise ye, and depart!' The morning rays
Lit up the emerald slope and crystal pool,
Sweet sustenance for many days,
And quiet resting places, calm and cool.
They knew not why, nor whither, yet they went!
His own hand put them forth, and so they were content.

And so they followed Him, they could not stay
When He had risen, the Shepherd good and fair.

. . . .

In pencil, May 1879.

Most Blessed For Ever.[1]

Psalm 21:6.

The prayer of many a day is all fulfilled,
Only by full fruition stayed and stilled;
You asked for blessing as your Father willed,
Now He hath answered: 'Most blessed for ever!'

[1] Written on her beloved father's death, but now chosen as the closing chord of F.R.H.'s songs on earth.

Lost is the daily light of mutual smile,
    You therefore sorrow now a little while;
But floating down life's dimmed and lonely aisle
    Comes the clear music: 'Most blessed for ever!'

From the great anthems of the Crystal Sea,
    Through the far vistas of Eternity,
Grand echoes of the word peal on for thee,
    Sweetest and fullest: 'Most blessed for ever!'

'And they sung as it were a new song before the throne.'—Revelation 14:3.

Index to First Lines.

Made in United States
Troutdale, OR
03/22/2024

18661504R00076